W9-ABY-852

A Study of Reciprocal Relations

BUREAU OF PUBLICATIONS

RELIGIOUS CONCERNS IN CONTEMPORARY EDUCATION

By PHILIP H. PHENIX

Dean, Carleton College

Teachers College, Columbia University

New York, 1959

Printed in the United States of America
LC: 59–11329

PREFACE

This brief study is intended as a contribution to the continuing discussion of the role of religion in contemporary education. It is directed chiefly to persons professionally concerned with education, both practitioners and students. It should also be of interest to lay people who take seriously their parental and civic responsibilities for education.

Many discussions about religion in education fall short because they presuppose a superficial and conventional conception of religion. The analysis offered in the following pages is based upon the more fundamental conception of religion as "ultimate concern"—a view having a prominent and respected place in contemporary religious thought as well as in the major religious traditions. This perspective makes it possible to grasp the underlying and governing principles of the educative process—as religious directives—in a manner not afforded by the more conventional outlook on religion.

The present study is offered as a suggested framework for thinking about religion and education in their reciprocal relations. It is the author's belief that fruitful understanding and intelligent action in this crucial domain of modern cultural life require a different orientation from that ordinarily adopted. This demands sustained attention to the inwardness and depth which are essential to spirituality rather than solely to the more obvious religious manifestations in beliefs, rites, and institutions.

The perspective here suggested should prove useful as a theoretical foundation for considering the place of religion in all types of schools—public and private, "religious" and "secular," lower and higher. It provides criteria for making distinctions appropriate to the several types of educational situations and for finding a way through the complex problems of interrelating church, state, and school.

If the reader gains from this analysis some sense of what it means to speak of education with religious foundations and some insight into the usefulness of this understanding in guiding contemporary educational policy, the objectives of the study will have been fulfilled.

P. H. P.

CONTENTS

RELIGIOUS CONCERNS IN CONTEMPORARY EDUCATION

A Study of Reciprocal Relations

1 RELIGION AND EDUCATION IN CONTEMPORARY CULTURE

OF all the concerns of mankind none are more profound and pervasive than religion and education. In all cultures and in every age men have held and celebrated beliefs about the sources and destinies of human life and about the powers that create and sustain the values that are most cherished. And in proportion to the depth and sincerity of these convictions there has been determination to transmit them to succeeding generations. Thus, between religion and education there is inevitably an intimate connection. Religion is concerned with dedication to whatever is deemed of fundamental and abiding worth, education with the process of bequeathing this treasure, intact if not improved, to the young.

The objective of this study is to discuss some of the interrelations of these two basic human concerns—religion and education—within the framework of modern culture. Underlying the analysis is the conviction that religion, properly understood, is both cornerstone and crown of education. It is the former because the entire educative endeavor is regulated by the governing life-orientation of the educator. It is the latter because education requires comprehensive objectives and commitments which it is the office of religion to provide. But the relationship between religion and education, though not symmetrical, is reciprocal. Education constitutes a test of religious commitment and provides occasions and contexts for expressing and implementing it. A person's real faith is revealed in what he is determined to instill in his children, and the controlling religious outlook of a community is embodied in the actual conduct of its educative institutions.

For this inquiry to be fruitful, it seems essential to employ an inclusive concept of religion and to consider religious experience as worthful yet in need of critical scrutiny. A narrow outlook would reduce the study to sectarian proportions. A general hostility to things religious would preclude any conclusion that education has in any sense religious foundations. An uncritical acceptance of historical forms of religion would be unintelligent and lacking in responsibility for the development of a richer and more secure conception of faith. Consequently it is assumed in all that follows that religion in the broad sense is an interesting and important factor in human life, and that it is not a closed and sacrosanct domain, but a living, growing complex of experience to which we may and ought to dedicate our best resources of intelligence and emotion.

Importance of the subject

Three factors in modern civilization render the study of religion in education of special importance. The first is the world-wide awakening of mankind to the importance of education. As never before in human history education has come to be regarded as an inalienable birthright. It is no longer considered to be the special privilege of a selected few who by fortune or inclination are accorded the advantages of learning. With education thus at the focus of attention, it has become natural to inquire by what faith it is governed and to what supreme goals it is directed. The more universal and central the significance of education, the closer it has moved toward the domain of religious conviction, i.e., concern for fundamental beliefs about the universe and man's place in it. The growing recognition that education is integral with realizing one's humanity has made urgent the problem of relating education to the faiths by which men live.

A second factor is the contemporary renewal of interest in religion. Modern man is in search of a faith. He is eagerly, even desperately, seeking for honest and dependable answers to questions about the meaning of life. He perceives the need for reliable foundations upon which to erect a secure yet creative civilization. Many of the traditional values and beliefs seem to have proven unsatisfactory, and it appears that new ones more adequate to the modern age must be discovered. In this seeking for faith education becomes a valued resource. Where might one better look for the clue to satisfying belief than in the activities of teaching and learning? Perhaps the very process of personal maturation—the day-by-day struggle of decision and creation—is the matrix out of which the living faith grows. If this is true, then not only is education guided by religious faith, but religion is in turn fashioned within the context of educational experience. It is therefore to be expected that the recent renewal of concern for religion would greatly stimulate interest in the relationships of religion and education.

Finally, both of the two preceding factors stem from a third, namely, the crisis in civilization through which mankind is now passing. Due largely to the rapid growth of industrialism the world over, established ways of life are being rudely shattered. Change, revolution, and reconstruction have become the order—and disorder—of the day. It is a time of troubles. Uncertainty and insecurity prevail. In such times men look to education and to religion for help. Both provide continuity with the past and some vision for the future. Both conserve the wisdom and inspiration of great men and hold aloft ideals for individuals and societies. In his time of crisis modern man looks to priest and prophet, to scholar and teacher, for some clue to the way he should go and the values and expectations he may entertain. It is then important that the guidance from religion and from education should as far as possible be compatible with each other and not serve merely to add to the reigning uncertainty and confusion. Hence the question of how these two great human enterprises are interrelated is of crucial significance in the contemporary cultural situation.

Evidences of concern for religion and education

Contemporary concern for the relations between education and religion is in evidence in many specific trends and movements. One of these is the ferment in the field of educational philosophy. Laymen and professionals alike are calling for a view of education in which the particularities of the teaching–learning process may be seen in relation to the most inclusive ends of life. Adherents of the several historic faiths are asking for educational programs which clearly express those faiths. There is a growing conviction that knowledge about effective methods of instruction and about the psychology of learning should not be divorced from fundamental purposes and beliefs, i.e., from basic religious orientations.

A second line of evidence is the remarkable revival of theological inquiry since the First World War. Most far-reaching has been the revolution in thought begun by the Swiss Protestant theologian Karl Barth, greatly stimulated by the rediscovery of the mid-nineteenth century Danish Christian Existentialist Soren Kierkegaard, and vigorously developed and transformed in America under the leadership of such men as Reinhold Niebuhr and Paul Tillich. There have been different but also notable contributions by such thinkers as Roman Catholic Jacques Maritain, Jewish Martin Buber, and Eastern Orthodox Nicolas Berdyaev.

These movements of thought are important chiefly because they constitute a protest against religious outlooks which have lost cultural perspective, either by becoming irrelevant to the real concerns of life or by becoming uncritically identified with existing patterns of secular life and thought. The critical theologians, working at the same time as believers, as scholars, and as educators, have sought to establish for modern man a vital connection between religious faith and the culture which it is the task of education to transmit and to enrich.

A third field of evidence is the active concern for religion in higher education, beginning in the 1920's. The National Council on Religion in Higher Education, established with a fellowship program for the purpose of improving the quality of instruction in religion in the universities, has since grown into a society of teachers, scholars, and administrators in many fields of specialization and in various types of institutions of higher education, who are dedicated to a religious outlook in the pursuit of their professional work.

Philanthropic foundations, notably the Edward W. Hazen Foundation and the Danforth Foundation, have given support and encouragement to the development of a religious orientation in higher education and have helped to attract into college teaching able young people with religious concerns. Through these and similar efforts, and as a consequence of the general thought movements of the times, as reflected in colleges and universities, the quality and scope of religious thought and instruction have notably increased, to the point where religious ideas are once again considered seriously in the academic community, as they rarely were a few decades ago.

Finally, there are many evidences of interest specifically in the problems of religion in the public schools. The Educational Policies Commission of the National Education Association has made a careful analysis of moral and spiritual values in public education and issued a report which has been widely studied. The Committee on Religion and Education of the American Council on Education, at work for more than a decade, has published in three important documents its findings on the place of religion in the public schools. The American Association of Colleges for Teacher Education, with the aid of the Danforth Foundation, has undertaken a series of pilot studies in several member institutions, designed to test ways of implementing in teacher training some of the recommendations of the earlier studies. Major religious bodies have from time to time made official declarations of position on the question of religion in public education. Many books about this problem by religious leaders, educators, and laymen have been published in recent years. Public discussions of the topic have been frequent and lively. Various practices involving religion in the schools have also been challenged in the courts, and some of the cases have even been carried to the U. S. Supreme Court to be decided on fundamental Constitutional principles.

These are some indications of the lively contemporary interest in the problems of relating religion and education. If the continuing debate is to be constructive, the issues should be clearly stated and thoughtfully considered. The present study is intended as a contribution to this end.

What is religion?

The most frequent source of confusion in discussions about religion and education is lack of clarity and consistency in the meaning of the concept "religion." It is therefore necessary, at the outset, to outline with as much precision as possible the significance of this central term.

The variety of descriptions. It is certain that we shall not be able to frame a simple, concise description of religion which will satisfy everybody. Many eminent thinkers have tried to suggest what they believed was the quintessence of religion, and formulations have varied widely. Kant, linking religion with morality, saw it as the rational conviction of a ground for the sense of obligation. Schleiermacher found the essence of religion in the feeling of absolute dependence. Durkheim and Macmurray saw the roots of religion in the consciousness of social relatedness, while Whitehead once referred to it as what man does with his solitariness. The naturalist, Dewey, considered religious experience as an outgrowth and expression of man's idealizing capacity, while supernaturalists have insisted that religion results from the self-disclosure of the personal God in historical revelation. Fromm has defined religion as a comprehensive system of life-orientation shared with a social group. Freud considered traditional religious beliefs as projections of infantile dependency wishes.

Some conceptions of religion, such as "belief in God," are definite and affirmative. Others are broader and more neutral, such as Brightman's view that religion is devotion to whatever is regarded as of supreme worth, together with the beliefs about the power or powers which create and sustain those values, or Benedict's view of religion as the experience of "wonderful power." Still other analyses consist largely of adverse judgments, such as Freud's mentioned above, Reinach's conception of religion as superstition impeding the free exercise of intelligence, and Marx's view of religion as "opiate of the people."

The variety of forms. Not only have many different conceptions of religion been formulated, but there is also a profusion of forms in which religion is expressed. In the first place, creedal forms vary. Some organized religions presuppose belief in many gods, others in one God; and a few have no deity at all. The divinity is most often regarded as personal, though in some religions it is conceived impersonally. Some creeds affirm a life after death, while others do not.

Secondly, institutional forms are of many kinds. Some religions are centered in the family, others create special religious communities, and a few emphasize the solitary individual. Church organization may be complex and centralized or simple and localized. In the third place, there are widely differing kinds of overt behavior associated with the various faiths. The rules of ethical conduct—concepts of moral law—give many different answers on such questions as sex relations, family responsibilities, treatment of enemies, slavery, civic obligations, and the distribution and uses of property. Ritual behavior, too, covers a wide range. Some worshippers celebrate their faith by shouting and dancing, others by silent meditation. Some engage in festive activity with bright color, rich pageantry, and abundant food and drink, while others express their conviction by ascetic renunciation of every sensory delight.

"Ultimacy" as the key to religion. In view of the many historic differences in descriptions and in forms of religion, is there any hope of gaining an adequate comprehensive conception with which to be guided in our study of the religious foundations of education? Some such conception there must be, else there would be no way of distinguishing the religious from the non-religious aspects or components of the educative process, and the discussion would produce only confusion.

In this study religion will be conceived of in terms of the idea of "ultimacy." In Paul Tillich's phrase, religion is that which concerns us ultimately. The non-religious is that which is of less than ultimate concern. While it cannot be claimed that this conception (which will presently be elaborated) fully satisfies all of the varying and frequently conflicting demands of the many historic descriptions and forms of religion, it is hoped that the ensuing discussions will demonstrate that the concept has both definiteness and inclusiveness, and affords considerable illumination of more traditional ways of understanding religion.

What, then, is meant by "ultimacy"? What is the significance of an ultimate concern, as contrasted with that which is less than ultimate? The following will help to make the concept clear.

1. *Importance.* The ultimate is the most important. Ultimate concern is belief or conduct in relation to whatever is considered of greatest importance. Religious experience has reference to matters of supreme moment. It is an affair of complete seriousness. This quality gives rise to the attitudes of awe and reverence which are traditionally associated with religious worship.

2. *Value.* Ultimacy further includes the ascription of supreme worth or value. This aspect is related to the sense of importance but is not identical with it. Value is importance personally perceived and appropriated. It is importance in relation to persons and not simply in objective generality. For example, the formation of the galaxies is a happening of great importance, yet because it is not perceived as directly associated with the personal life of the one who makes such a judgment it would not ordinarily be called an event of great value. An individual's choice of a life-work or of a marriage partner, on the other hand, would on the cosmic scene be of little importance, but from the standpoint of the person concerned a wise choice in either case would be a matter of great importance and hence of high value.

Furthermore, importance is neutral as between good and evil, while value is not. Thus, disease and death are as important as health and birth, yet the former and the latter are of different value. The religious consciousness is aware of those matters of importance, both good and evil, which evoke the response of wonder, awe, and amazement, but it goes beyond these attitudes to judgments of value—to affirmation or denial of worth. Hence the religious outlook is concerned with grading matters of supreme importance in scales of relevance to persons and of good and evil.

3. *Depth.* In addition to importance and value, ultimacy

refers to depth. Ultimate concern probes beneath the surface of things to the deeper significance. It does not rest content with appearances. The religious person does not take his life experiences at face value but tries to discern the more profound meanings and purposes to which they point. A superficial, literal outlook does not satisfy him. Ultimate concern leads one to ask the most searching questions, to face the most perplexing difficulties, to push the inquiry to the boundary where knowledge shades off into mystery, rational belief into faith, and comfortable assurance into hope. Ultimacy has reference to experience at the limits of the ordinary. Religion as ultimate concern is the serious personal encounter with the boundaries of human existence. It means living in the vivid awareness of the final limitations which condition the human situation.

4. *Totality*. The ultimate also has the aspect of totality or comprehensiveness. Every experience which seeks to be utterly inclusive moves toward ultimacy. A person's ultimate concern is his relation to the totality of existence. Religion is one's comprehensive life-orientation. It is what one makes of his life as a whole. Ultimacy in this respect is in contrast with all that is partial, one-sided, or fragmentary. The religious outlook is in evidence whenever a person seeks seriously and unceasingly for inclusiveness and completeness, not being satisfied with particular goods or special goals. Religion thus involves a reaching out for the infinite.

5. *Origins*. One kind of question which is characteristic of ultimate concern is that of origin or source. It is characteristic of most if not all religious faiths to contain some affirmations about how the world came into existence, the sources of its continued being, and particularly the ground of individual personality. Beliefs about world creation, providence, and the making of souls are important features of the historic religions. Inquiries into such matters are a consequence of the drive toward depth and comprehensiveness of understanding, in relation to temporal and causal factors.

6. *Destinies.* Similar to the concern for origins but prospective rather than retrospective in outlook is the concern for destinies or ends which is another aspect of ultimacy. Religion not only contains beliefs about the grounds from which the world of existing things emerges but also about the consummation toward which all things tend. Thus the great religions have had something to say about the problem of death, hopes for life after death, and rewards and punishments at a final day of accounting. Just as the demand for ultimacy in relation to the past leads to a search for the creative source, so ultimate concern in respect to the future prompts a venture of expectant faith about the outcomes of personal and cosmic development.

7. *Relationship.* Finally, ultimacy is expressed in the search for relationships. Depth and comprehensiveness operate not only with reference to beginnings and endings but also to the connections in between. The ultimate significance of existence is understood only as individual entities and experiences are comprehended within some kind of coherent pattern. Origin is not just the starting point but also the path leading to the present. Destiny is not merely the conclusion but also the direction to be travelled in reaching fulfillment. Convictions about what is most important and what is supremely valuable apply not primarily to things but to relationships. The ultimate in knowledge, generally called truth, is a complex of connections between individual entities drawn together into unified conceptual schemes. Thus religion traditionally raises questions and makes affirmations about such matters as the right Way of Life, the Will of God, Natural Law, and the Truth. All of these illustrate ultimate concern for relationships.

The occasions for ultimacy. We have now indicated the basic meanings of ultimacy, and have shown their relevance to some of the recurrent concerns of traditional religion. To clarify the concept further a few words may be helpful regarding the occasions for ultimacy. How and when does ultimacy enter into experience? Much of life is lived on a less than ultimate level. Most ordinary happenings are comparatively unimportant, superficial, and partial, relate to matters of less than supreme value, and do not concern origins, destiny, or comprehensive relationships. Under what circumstances, then, does the extraordinary quality of ultimacy—and thus, by definition, of religious consciousness—come into play? Three main types of occasions may be suggested.

1. *Inquiry.* Man's intelligence is by nature restless. It breaks the bonds of the purely customary and routine. Reason pushes out beyond the realm of the familiar to explore new possibilities. Imagination leaps beyond the well-worn patterns of thought to more inclusive and more illuminating ideas. The multiplicity of experience cries out for coordination and the apparently fortuitous calls for explanation.

Inquiry is a pathway toward ultimacy. It is founded upon a sense of the important, is guided by convictions of value, seeks to probe beyond appearances, aims at generality, and explores causes, consequences, and connections. Ultimacy is experienced whenever inquiry is pursued to its limits, seriously, ceaselessly, and courageously. Such inquiry gives rise to the intellectual component in religion. Man is by nature rational, and the full and insistent employment of his intellect is religious in quality.

2. *Desire.* Human beings are also creatures of emotion. Life has a subjective intensity manifest in desire. The quality of existence is felt rather than thought. Furthermore, desire has no bounds. Biological needs may be satisfied but human desire, unlike mere animal appetite, is never fulfilled. Just as thought leaps off toward the infinite, so does the gaining of one object of desire but suggest new riches to be gained.

It is this infinitude of desire which makes it an occasion for ultimacy. Deep yearnings are obviously grounded in convictions about what is most significant and valuable. Hopes and longings probe beyond the merely apparent and struggle for completeness. Emotional life seeks confirmation in primordial sources and in expected outcomes, the quality of relationships is perceived in the life of feeling. Religious experience thus partakes of emotion as well as of intellect. Whenever the spirit of man manifests itself in desires forever unsatisfied there is an occasion of religious significance.

3. *Decision.* Ultimacy is approached in act as well as in inquiry and desire. Man is free and he must decide what he will do and who he will be. He is faced with innumerable possibilities of conduct, and he is required to make a choice among them.

Nothing is more important to a person than his own life, since that is all he has. Thus decisions which determine who one will be are in the nature of the case ultimate. The decisions one makes are also a reflection of his real values. In the long run what a person truly prizes most will be made evident in conduct. Serious decisions demand fundamental thinking based on a consideration of the entire range of relevant factors. Every choice is itself in part a beginning and yet is made in the light of precedent acts. Each decision is also based upon some consideration of personal destiny and of the relationships which make possible some advances toward the goal. In all of these respects, therefore, decisions provide occasions for the experience of religion as ultimacy. Thus to the intellectual and emotional approaches to religion is added that of volition.

The symbols of ultimacy. In the foregoing paragraphs religion has been defined as ultimate concern, and ultimacy has been further elaborated in several directions. It may be objected that this definition is too abstract and too different from the everyday understanding involving such things as churches, creeds, priests, bibles, and rituals. Actual religious life is indeed more specific and concrete than any general definition such as "ultimate concern" can suggest. But its forms are the special outward manifestations of the inner ultimacy. They are the symbols of ultimacy, reflecting the many ways in which religion becomes elaborated in concrete historical existence.

Religious beliefs—creeds, theologies, religious philosophies—are systems of concepts which have been designed to express the ultimate concerns of individuals and groups. Religious institutions, with their many ways of determining membership and of exercising authority, are social expressions of ultimate concern. Similarly, the several moral codes and countless ritual systems of mankind are means approved by the various groups for embodying ultimate concerns in overt action.

The mind, heart, and inner being of religion is ultimacy, but this spiritual reality must be incorporated. If thoughts, feelings, and intentions are to have effect, endurance, and social relevance, they must find concrete expression. The point of crucial importance is that the symbols of ultimacy should not be taken as the aim and substance of religion itself. The external manifestations should always be understood in the light of the ultimacies they are designed to incorporate. The sole reason for existence of the outward forms is to point to an inward reality.

Yet here arises a problem of central importance. The forms of ultimacy are often empty. The symbols of religion may become detached from the spiritual reality they were created to represent and may pursue an independent existence. Thus it comes to pass that for many people, if not for most, religion simply and solely means acknowledging beliefs (even though their significance is not understood), belonging to a church, reading sacred writings, and performing certain specified ritual acts. The externals thus become for many the identifying characteristics of religion, while the inner reality which called them into being and which is their primary justification is neglected. It is for this reason that religion as commonly understood and practiced may be a matter of comparatively minor importance, valued far less than the pursuit of pleasure, power, or knowledge, and without penetration or depth. It may become a special department of life rather than a comprehensive orientation, and may have scant reference to the grounds, the ends, or the pervasive relationships and meanings of life. In short, customary religion may be far removed from ultimate concern.

This degeneration of religious symbols into empty forms is a major cause of difficulty and confusion in describing and discussing religion. The role of ultimate concern in human life is obviously in sharpest contrast with that of specialized formal pursuits such as subscribing to a creed or belonging to a religious organization. When the same word "religion" is then used both in relation to ultimacy and to its detached symbols, misunderstandings and conflicts are to be expected.

Nevertheless, both the ultimacy and its expressions belong to religion. Even though the symbols can become separated from their proper referents, they still pertain to them and when rightly interpreted may regain their symbolic power. An important approach to better understanding in religion is therefore to strengthen or re-establish the weakened or broken connections between ultimate concerns and their external forms. Theological formulas, holy books, ritual acts, and sacred institutions—which in popular understanding *are* religion—need to be examined in the light of their historical origins and their meaning in the lives of those who by common consent have been the exemplars of the faith, to reveal the ultimate concerns which these symbols are meant to represent. Similarly, ultimate concerns should be considered with respect to the varieties of forms which can effectively symbolize them.

This two-way consideration of the relations between ultimate concerns and their symbolic expressions will be the basic approach throughout this study. The method is founded on the conviction that the experience of ultimacy—the concern for supreme importance, value, depth, comprehensiveness, origins, destinies, and relationships—is the proper core and inner meaning of religion and also that this sense of ultimacy must become manifest in words, deeds, and institutions. In particular, the religious foundations of education can fruitfully be explored in relation to both the outer and the inner aspects of religion, the symbols and the spirit which gives them life.

Education and religion compared

Education shares with religion a position of basic significance in human life. As in the case of religion, many different meanings have been assigned to the term "education." Some have claimed all of life as the province of education. Others have designated as educative only those aspects of experience which promote learning, or growth leading to still further growth. Some describe education as transmission of culture, others as the molding of young persons in adult patterns. There are descriptions which emphasize individual development, while others are based on the concept of social interaction. Education is commonly regarded as that which occurs or ought to occur in schools; more sophisticated conceptions recognize the many other agencies and informal means through which teaching and learning take place.

Despite the many different emphases in defining the province of education, there would seem to be general agreement that it is concerned fundamentally with influences affecting the development and maturation of persons, either for their own sakes or to embody a social heritage. There are conflicting goals, methods, and theories of education, but no such profound differences of basic understanding as are present in the case of religion. Education may be directed toward self-realization, or adjustment, or social efficiency. It may take place in schools or homes, in a group or in solitude, by reading books or making things with one's hands or participating in a committee meeting. Yet in all its forms some kind of personal development is intended.

Like religion, education has both inner substance and outward manifestations. There is the central educational reality of personal transformation, and there are the various ideas, institutions, and practices which are designed to provide visible evidence for the educative process. Fortunately, and in contrast with religion, the primary purpose—human development—is seldom lost sight of in the pursuit of externals. To be sure, some meaningless pedagogical routines do come to be regarded as education itself. Attending school, reading books, and listening to lectures—the mechanics of education—are often mistakenly assumed as guarantees that education is occurring. But these illusions have not been so persistent, so widespread, or so deeply rooted as the corresponding ones in the case of religion. It has been generally recognized that underlying the words, the institutions, and the activities of educators, there is a deliberate intention of assisting the maturation of human personality, whether for individual or for social ends. The forms of the educative process have seldom become independent and self-justifying activities, without any clear relation to the essential educative intention.

Education has been able better than religion to maintain its integrity—its life-giving union of inward substance and outward expression—because education is for the most part concerned with finite experience. Religion, on the other hand, is concerned with ultimacy, which represents man's commerce with infinitude. In its inner substance and intention religion concerns the infinite, but its outward expressions are necessarily finite. The split between the inner and the outer occurs when the finite forms are taken literally, at face value, rather than as symbols pointing beyond themselves to the ultimate. Education differs in this respect fundamentally, in that the finite forms of instruction can be direct and literal translations of finite educative intentions.

Education and ultimacy

Religion is fundamental to education to the extent that the latter occurs within the context of ultimate concern. Most teaching and learning concern matters of less than ultimate significance and thus are not directly of a religious quality. But the educative process is implicitly governed by a set of basic convictions which are of a religious nature, and hence education is at least indirectly linked to ultimacy.

Let us consider in turn the several aspects of ultimacy described earlier in the chapter. In the long run the teacher will communicate what he regards as most important, and the learner will grow in directions which are of most vital concern to himself. Thus convictions about what is most important will determine the relative interest in and emphasis on various types of learning experience. Similarly, the guidance of human development necessarily presupposes a scale of values. Preferred directions will be encouraged, while tendencies regarded as evil will be avoided. The scale of values reveals which matters are considered of supreme worth and which are regarded with greatest disapproval. The making of educational decisions is thus implicitly guided by convictions about ultimate values.

It is also characteristic of education to seek depth. Certainly in the field of intellectual inquiry maximum depth is a classic scholarly ideal. The well-educated person has learned not to make hasty and ill-founded judgments; he has the wisdom to probe beneath superficial appearances. Inclusiveness is another characteristic education objective. The ideal educated man is complete, well-rounded, many-sided, whole. Thus profundity and completeness, two further aspects of ultimacy, are fundamental to education.

The process of influencing human development also involves matters of origin and destiny. The very idea of growth presupposes both origination and goals. In changing personality new powers arise, and the question of the sources and conditions of creation becomes pertinent. The educator cannot escape the problem of the grounds for creative advance, for that is what he himself through his teaching work wishes to encourage and assist. He must also have aims, or purposes, and these necessarily reflect some conviction about human destiny, about the ends toward which the whole developmental process moves or should move.

Finally, the educator bases his activities upon an awareness of relationships. He seeks to guide human lives into meaningful, harmonious patterns of existence. The fulfillment of being involves the discovery of mutual compatibilities and possible coordinations. Success and satisfaction in directing the process of growth depend on recognizing and using the connections between the manifold elements of experience. In this way also education takes place within the context of ultimacy.

Religion as ultimate concern therefore provides the large framework within which education occurs. It determines perspective and basic orientation. It governs emphasis and fixes trends. Religious concern (whether or not recognized and designated as such) is the motive which actuates the educator and produces the general pattern of his work. The relationship between education and religion as ultimate concern is, in fact, a reciprocal one. Not only does religion provide the ultimate foundation for education, but education provides an admirable field for implementing religious commitments, thus making faith explicit in concrete act. A significant test of the governing religious convictions of a person or group is the character of the education promoted by that person or group.

2 RELIGION AND THE SCHOOL

SCHOOLS are the institutions deliberately and formally established to provide education. They are the regular and ordinary means for promoting human development within a social and cultural heritage. They are civilized inventions designed to insure continuity of tradition. The concern of schools is with education corporately conceived, just as religious institutions afford corporate expression of religious faith. However, while churches are formal crystallizations of ultimate concerns, schools are the concrete social embodiment of ordinary cultural concerns, which for the most part are not ultimate. The question of the religious foundations of the school arises when one asks how these ordinary, less than ultimate, concerns are related to the ultimates by which the lives of individuals and groups are governed.

The distinction between education and schools and the distinction between religion and religious institutions are important to any clear understanding of the issues under discussion. The relation of education to religion is not the same as that of education to the churches. Nor is either of these identical with the relation of religion to the school or of the school to the church.

Matters are further complicated by the fact that both schools and religious institutions function within a social order with established agencies of government. A distinction parallel to that applicable to both religion and education is thus required with respect to society. Corresponding to the comprehensive and vital realities called "religion" (as ultimate concern) and "education" (as the guidance of personal growth) there is "society" as the web of mutual accommodations and adjustments which make possible and fruitful the life in association with others. Corresponding to the institutional embodiments of religion and education in churches and schools are the laws, customs, and agencies of government which may be collectively designated as the "state." The state is the concrete and visible expression of the social order. Yet the established civic institutions may and frequently do in time cease to reflect the inner realities of social cohesion, assuming an autonomous existence devoid of functional meaning. When this happens, the connection between society and state may need to be re-established by the creation of new laws and institutions to replace the obsolete ones or by modifying and reinterpreting the old instrumentalities in the light of new social conditions.

An adequate consideration of religion and education within the social context must take account of these three distinctions: religion and church, education and school, society and state. As indicated in the following diagram, a variety of interrelationships exist, based on the possible combinations of terms. For example, the problem of church and state is not the same as that of religion and state. Thus, there may be questions of ultimate concern about the government

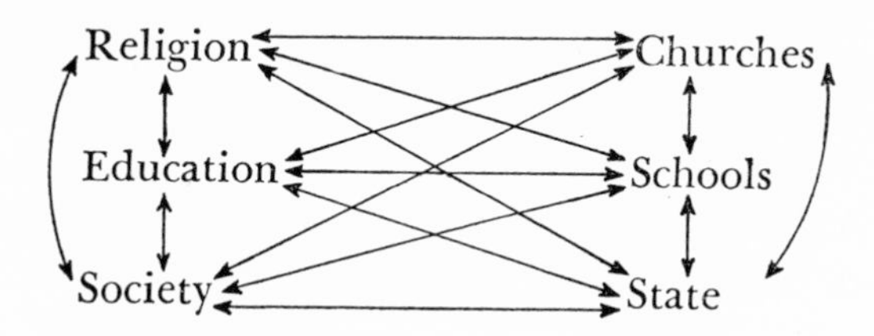

of a nation, but these concerns may find no expression in the institutional forms of religion. Nor is the problem of religion and state the same as that of religion and society, since the realities of social order may not be faithfully reflected in the institutions of government. Again, questions of religion and education are not identical with those of religion and schools, nor are the relations of education and the churches equivalent to those of schools and churches.

Much confusion could be avoided if these distinctions were kept in view in discussing religion and education within the social context. The character of the relationships depends to a considerable degree upon whether the terms are employed in the broad or narrow, inner or outer, sense. Difficulties and inconsistencies often occur because the contrasting meanings are used interchangeably and without change of designation within a single discussion.

In this chapter our attention is focused on the school, as the formal institution of education, and its relationships to religion and religious institutions. On the basis of the foregoing analysis, three major types of schools may be described, with respect to their religious foundations.

The secular school

The word "secular," like the word "religious," has more than one meaning. One common and useful meaning is: "not under the authority of a religious institution and not concerned with ecclesiastical or theological matters." In this sense secular institutions are those which are free of any ties to organized religion, and secular studies are those which do not deal with theological or ecclesiastical matters. A secular school is one established or controlled under other auspices than those of organized religion. This conception of the secular school corresponds to the conventional rather than to the fundamental meaning of religion. The secular school in this sense is distinguished from the church school.

There is also a broader meaning of secular, which corresponds to the inclusive conception of religion as ultimate concern. The secular in this second sense is used to contrast with the sacred. Secular affairs are those of less than ultimate concern, and a secular school is one in which the teaching and learning involve matters of limited significance. Objectives are specific and circumscribed, inquiries remain within the domain of the clear and comprehensible, avoiding the depths of mystery, ineffability, and paradox. The program of such a school is wholly devoted to the many special interests and activities which arise out of everyday life, with its ordinary occupational, recreational, and civic demands. The curriculum is simply a collection of learning experiences designed to meet the many particular needs of civilized life.

What are the religious foundations of secular schools? Are there ultimate concerns which underlie them? Such institutions are created and controlled by people who do have ultimate concerns, and the nature of these commitments affects the program of the school. In a school which is secular in the narrower, conventional sense there may, of course, be ultimate concerns directly and explicitly built into the educational program, even though they are not expressed by traditional belief systems or institutional relationships. Such schools belong in the category of intrinsically religious schools (in the fundamental sense) to be discussed below. On the other hand, schools which are secular in the fundamental sense merely reflect in a more or less haphazard way the various concerns of the individuals and groups that make use of them. To clarify the relation of secular schools to these external religious factors, three relatively distinct kinds of secular educational programs may be noted.

Ad hoc programs. Many schools offer courses of study simply in response to particular demands. If in a certain locality at a given time sufficient interest is expressed in English language instruction for foreign-born people, or in basket-weaving, or in the religions of mankind, courses of study in these subjects may be provided. The basic belief systems out of which these interests grow and of which they are partial evidence differ from one person to the next. The course offerings are *ad hoc,* contingent upon the chance aggregation of demands arising from a variety of individuals each with his own peculiar life-pattern. The program of the school is thus not a manifestation of any coherent set of convictions, and may thus scarcely be said to have religious foundations in any significant or definite sense.

Organized private interest programs. Other secular schools serve the interests of certain organized interest groups. Many private schools, for example, are dedicated to the maintenance and advancement of the way of life of one social or economic class. The whole school program is organized around the values which are most prized by the members of such a self-conscious segment of society. The private interests which support and control such schools possess more or less clearly defined ultimate concerns, and it is these commitments which constitute the religious foundations of the schools.

Public school programs. The school may derive its ultimate values neither from individuals only nor from organized private interests but from the needs and interests of society as a whole or of its majority groups. The public philosophy is seldom as sharply defined as that of private interest groups, largely because it is compounded of many relatively independent and often conflicting tendencies which must be welded into a tolerable and practicable compromise. Nonetheless, there are certain basic policies and persuasions of society as a whole which govern the conduct of public education. In the United States, for example, the public schools would be expected to inspire the young with the ideals of American democracy as embodied in American traditions and as expressed in such documents as the Declaration of Independence, the Constitution, and the Bill of Rights. Concepts like inalienable natural rights, equality before the law, the fundamental human freedoms, and the dignity of the individual are elements in an American Creed which affirms the values to which the public is, in principle at least, supremely dedicated.

The ultimacy which underlies the public school program in other cases may not reflect certain common affirmations of justice and right, such as those just cited, but may be comprised of supreme devotion to the state itself. The state, as the explicit institutional expression of social unity and power, is then not regarded as deriving its ideals and authority from a more fundamental source of social value, but as constituting the highest value in its own being. In such cases, as illustrated in totalitarian social systems, the public philosophy is identified with governmental policy, and the public schools exist solely to serve the deified state (i.e., the political organization as the object of ultimate concern).

The contrast between the above two types of religious foundations for secular public schools illustrates the importance of distinguishing between society and the state. A school program founded upon the ultimate ideals of society (as in a commitment to certain standards of justice) differs in many respects, in content and spirit, from one based upon absolute loyalty to the state. In both cases the belief systems by which the school is guided are derived from beyond the school itself, and both are public in nature, but direction by public moral conscience is very different from conformity to government regulation.

The church school

A second main type of school is the church school, that is, a school which serves the interests of some organized religious body. Church schools are distinguished from secular schools in the narrower sense defined above. When it comes to the more fundamental meaning of secular, however, a certain ambiguity arises. It is quite possible for a church school to be secular in the basic sense that its program is not concerned with ultimates. For example, an organized religious body may operate a school designed solely to prepare farmers, mechanics, lawyers, business men, or housewives, without reference to the meaning of these occupations within a comprehensive scheme of dedication and destiny. The program of such a school may differ in no major respect from the educational operations of any other private interest group such as a woman's club or a labor union.

Furthermore, a church school can be secular in the fundamental sense even when it provides instruction in so-called religious matters. If the subject matter of religious teaching is simply a specialized discipline, one among the several particular areas of knowledge or practice to be studied, it is not an object of ultimate concern and therefore not religious in the comprehensive sense. Even church schools which are designed to prepare professional religious leaders may discharge their functions in an essentially secular fashion, by training the students merely as technical experts in the handling of formally sacred beliefs and acts.

This basic secularism of some church schools is usually the result of the prior routinizing or fossilizing of the life of the religious organizations which the schools serve. Institutional beliefs and practices have become literal and autonomous. They have lost their symbolic reference to and connection with the ultimate concern which gave them birth and supplies their only sufficient justification. Thus secularized church schools simply bear the marks of an ultimacy which they can no longer claim in fact but only in name.

On the other hand, there are church schools which do maintain a living relationship to the ultimate concerns of the fostering religious community. In these schools not only the program of religious studies but the entire educational effort is fashioned to accord with and advance the accepted faith. The religious foundations of these schools are derived from the organized community of believers and the educational program serves the propagation of their living faith.

The intrinsically religious school

Both of the above types of schools—the secular school and the church school—look beyond themselves for their ultimate sources of value and dedication. The secular school reflects the belief systems of individuals, of special interest groups, of society as a whole, or of the holders of political power. The church school is based upon the governing convictions of an organized religious body. In both cases the ultimate religious foundations are extrinsic and derived.

The third major type of school differs from the first two in having a religious basis intrinsic to the very life of the school itself, in having an original rather than a derived ultimacy. The intrinsically religious school exists whenever the educative process itself becomes the occasion for asking the most profound questions, entertaining the highest hopes and expectations, and making the most basic decisions. The school is intrinsically religious when beliefs about what is most important, supremely worthful, most real, primordial, eternal, and meaningful are not borrowed from a sphere of life beyond the school but arise directly from life within the school. Teaching and learning activities are regarded not as specialized pursuits deriving their character and justification elsewhere, but as unique opportunities for apprehending the most profound significance of human existence.

In the intrinsically religious school it is not assumed that instruction must always remain on the level of special, particular, and circumscribed fact, theory, and skill, and that questions about the comprehensive, about the mysteries at the limits of finitude, about the personal response to existence as a whole, must always be referred to persons and agencies—theologians and churches—charged with responsibility for these larger interests. It is presupposed rather that such inquiries are of the essence of education, seriously conceived, and that convictions or ideas gained from pursuing them are appropriate and desirable fruits of learning.

The intrinsically religious school presupposes a conception of religion as directly relevant to every human activity rather than as a specialized interest appropriate only to certain designated persons and institutions. According to this view, family life, occupational pursuits, life as a citizen, and recreation, for example, may be intrinsically religious in character, just as the school may be. None of these experiences need to derive their religious significance from beyond themselves. It is from within these very activities, engaged in with full seriousness, that ultimate concerns originate. School life thus takes its place with the other common experiences as an occasion for ultimacy.

Yet the religious situation of the school in relation to original or derivative quality is in two respects exceptional. On the one hand, the school is commonly regarded as an instrument created to serve society. To perpetuate its life, each community must transmit its cultural achievements from generation to generation by education. The school is the primary means for effecting this cultural continuity. The community seeks to insure its persistence through local public schools, the nation through national schools, special interest groups through private schools, and religious organizations through church schools. In each case the school is regarded as the servant of the social group which creates and maintains it. It follows that schools are expected to derive their goals from beyond themselves. This is why the religious foundations of formal education have so generally been extrinsic rather than original and intrinsic.

On the other hand, despite this instrumental character of educational institutions, they are uniquely fitted to provide creative leadership for the societies which they have been formed to serve. A school does not effectively fulfill its mission to society by obediently duplicating the life of the present adult generation in the young entrusted to it. Educators ought not to be merely social mechanics who build the new generation by following a blueprint supplied by others. Teachers are also living, responsible members of society, with an opportunity not only to transmit culture but to improve it.

Furthermore, the life of the school is not borrowed or imported from outside. It has its own being and validity. It is not justified only as it reproduces or represents conditions of life in the community beyond itself. School experience has its own meaning, which may in turn have redemptive significance for persons and institutions outside the school.

Schools in fact have both derivative and originative functions. It would be as wrong for the school to attempt to create a wholly new society as to care only for the exact duplication of the existing order. Creation and transmission are complementary functions. The school can have a life of its own only because it has been well supplied with cultural resources not of its own making. But it can transmit the past effectively not as inert stuff but only as a tradition which has entered into the very being of living persons, and in this incorporation has been both conserved and transformed.

While these principles of originality and derivation for the schools and culture are of wider application, they have been introduced here with specific reference to the sources of ultimacy. The essential point is that the religious insights which apply to experience in the school do not need to be imported from outside sources, such as the churches or the state. These may provide valuable support and fruitful suggestions concerning the ultimacies appropriate to school life, but even what is imported, if it is to be vital, must be rediscovered within and made relevant to the educational experience.

Intrinsically religious schools must clearly have a considerable degree of independence. If the sense of what is most important and of supreme value is to be implicit in the school experience, educational policy must not be prescribed in detail from outside. Only if there is freedom to let inquiry, expectation, and decision carry the members of the educational community into the heights and depths as occasion demands, can there be authentic original experiences of ultimacy. The school may in practice be under the control of either public or private agencies and yet be granted fundamental autonomy in the discovery of its own most profound spiritual resources and commitments. Thus the nominal arrangements for the determination of school policy do not in themselves indicate whether or not the school is intrinsically religious. The crucial condition for original ultimacy is simply that the educational policy, by whatever agency determined, include a large grant of freedom to the academic community to discover its own roots.

Religious foundations for schools in a pluralistic society

The distinctions between secular, church, and intrinsically religious schools are of special importance in a pluralistic culture such as that of the United States. Every society must allow for differences in the individuals and groups of which it is composed. No society, because of the principle of differentiation upon which it is founded, can exist with everyone alike. And every social group provides not only for functional differences but also for a certain degree of arbitrary personal variation. But all societies at the same time require unifying factors. The functional differences must be articulated into some sort of effective cooperation for the common good. Destructive conflicts must be minimized. Joint efforts presuppose some basis in values held in common.

The fundamental problem of all social life is that of unity and diversity. How can the differences between persons, alone or in association, be employed so as to enrich rather than impoverish the life of the community? Indeed, how can these truly be a community at all—a unity of contrasting persons and groups? The problem of the creation of community is essentially a religious one, since the most fundamental issues of value, of decision, of meaning, and of relationship arise in connection with it. The crucial test of the ability to create community is the existence of many diverse cultures and traditions within the society, i.e., the condition of pluralism. When there is a single uniform and well-established way of life for a people, social cohesion is easily maintained. But when, through migrations and rapid social change, people with widely differing customs and beliefs are brought together as members of the same society, a basis for the common life must be found on a deeper level than the ideas and habits which govern everyday activity. It is this necessity of discovering a foundation comprehensive enough and deep enough to establish unity among the diverse elements of a plural society that marks community-making as a religious problem.

Government as a source of unity. There are three principal institutions through which the required unity for a pluralistic society may be provided. The first and most obvious of these is government. In some societies, obligations and loyalties to the state take precedence over any contrary requirements of private conviction. Laws and the authorities designated to administer them give detailed expression to the rules by which the many become one. The requirements of citizenship are taught to the young in schools conducted under state supervision. The greater the social differences to be harmonized, the stronger must be the authority of government. When internal discord or threat from without endangers the integrity of a people, it may prove necessary to institute drastic governmental regulations which greatly curtail the freedom of individuals and groups to follow their private convictions. In such highly regulated states plurality virtually disappears in favor of uniformity by government decree.

Organized religion as a source of unity. The second means of achieving social unity is through organized religion. Such unity as was achieved among the many different cultures of Europe in the Middle Ages was within the framework of the supra-national Roman Catholic Church. Even today that world-wide church binds together in common loyalty and faith peoples of many races, nations, and tongues. The non-Roman Christians—Protestant and Eastern Orthodox—likewise aspire to found a universal Christian commonwealth, and have already demonstrated some degree of institutional unity in the establishment of the World Council of Churches. The rise of Islam was associated with spectacular success in the unification of hitherto isolated or warring desert tribes, and within a brief period this relatively simple and practical faith became the basis for a far-flung Islamic empire. Once again in the twentieth century the Muslim religion is experiencing a revival and is being looked to as a source of unity for Arab peoples and eventually for all mankind.

The case is similar for all of the great organized religions. Each has provided a powerful basis for social cohesion. The faith of Israel, based on the one sacred Torah, has for more than two and half millenia maintained the integrity of a people widely dispersed and bitterly persecuted, yet ever and again creating new centers of life and civilization wherever they have settled. Likewise in the Far East, Hinduism and Buddhism, each with several branches and sects, have bound into a common family of faith millions of adherents scattered over wide geographical areas and divided by language and custom.

Schools are an important means of propagating these unifying faiths. In fact, whenever the unity of a society is based upon adherence to an organized religion, formal education is vested in the religious authorities. The official teaching of the Roman Catholic Church is that the entire education of Catholic children should be under the supervision of the Church, to which the supreme teaching authority has been given by God. The impetus for popular education in modern times was partly due to the efforts of Protestants to instruct all believers in the reading of the Bible. Teaching has traditionally been a central function of the synagogue, and Muslim education has been centered in the mosque and in specifically Islamic universities. In Hindu civilization the teacher, or *guru,* is a member of the Brahman or priestly caste, and in Buddhist cultures virtually all instruction is provided by monks in the monasteries.

Schools as a source of unity. In addition to the state and organized religion, the third possible basis for social unity is the system of formal education—the institution of the school. When social cohesion is produced by political power or by adherence to one organized religion, the school takes its place as a subordinate agency serving the ends of state or church. If the school itself serves as the unifying foundation, it no longer has to take its cues from these other institutions, but provides direction for society out of its own resources. The whole educational system, ranging from the most advanced research institutes to the play school, constitutes a primary means of cultural creation, assimilation, criticism, conservation, and transmission.

The school can contribute in a major way to social unity only when formal education is widespread. Universal education is a recent phenomenon in the history of mankind. Only in the twentieth century has it become a reality in some of the leading nations of the world. In many places it remains only an ideal. May it not be that the spread of educational opportunity has ushered in a new era in the history of mankind through affording a different and potentially more effective basis for cultural integration than could be provided by either the state or organized religion? Is the universal community of teaching and learning a new institutional arrangement for bringing together into a constructive unity the contrasting and often conflicting ideas and activities of mankind?

In outlining the above three institutional sources of unity—the state, religious organizations, and schools—the case has been to some extent over-simplified. In the first place there are other institutions, such as the family and occupational associations, which must be taken into account. These were not considered as basic, however, because unlike the state, a dominant church, or a system of universal education, they tend to be sources of difference rather than of unity. Secondly, social unity at the deepest level is not provided by institutions but by pervasive common ideals and values in individual persons. Thus, what Gunnar Myrdal calls "the American Creed" is a set of widespread and deeply rooted convictions about freedom, equality, and individual rights which are brought to bear in a variety of ways in many different activities of life, both public and private. Though formalized in declarations, constitutions, laws, and court decisions, these uniting beliefs are not simply government regulations. Nor are they the explicit faith of an organized religious body or of the educational community. They are generally accepted and largely unquestioned moral persuasions which have relevance in all democratic life. In the third place, there is no single unifying agency in a society. It is never the state, the church, or the school alone which binds the community together. Each social institution may contribute in its own way to the creation of a commonwealth. Cooperation toward shared objectives gives the best promise of a productive and stable social order.

With these qualifications in mind, let us return to the principal theme—the role of the school in a pluralistic culture. The state has played and still plays an important role in social coordination in the United States. Religious institutions, on the other hand, in a pluralistic society like this one, are more a source of diversity than of unity. The educational system, and particularly the public school system, has been a unifying factor. In looking to the future we cannot escape the questions: Where does the best promise lie for the fulfillment of man's highest values? Is there hope for the creation of a universal community wherein all the peoples of the earth in their individuality and variety may realize their supreme good? Some would deny the possibility of a commonwealth of man as a utopian dream. Others would look for the eventual establishment of a world government. Still others expect the consummation to come within one of the historic religious bodies, whose universal claims will at length be made good.

Perhaps the educational enterprise is the best answer of all to the problem of bringing diverse kinds of persons and groups into a constructive unity. In principle the teaching–learning community is committed to the examination and assessment of the whole range of human experience. There is nothing in all the worlds of actuality or possibility, of realization or imagination, which falls beyond the concern of the academic world. This does not imply that any student or any teacher may appropriately at any given time engage in any given kind of inquiry. Order, conditions, and priorities must be respected in the search for truth. Still, the community of scholarship, considered as a whole, is ready to assume the task of bringing meaning to the entire complex of human experience.

This educational ideal of comprehensive assimilation and coordination is an ultimate concern, and enables the school as an institution to claim a more fundamental position than either the state or the organized religious bodies. The state deals with the outward regulation of public life, and has hardly begun to solve the problem of a world community. Social unity grounded in governmental power is either arbitrary and oppressive or it is derivative from widely accepted cultural values for which the institutions of education are a major source and channel. Organized religion, while at its best far more deeply concerned than government with the inward springs of personal and social life, has not been able to reconcile all the competing belief systems and diverse cultural traditions of contemporary civilization.

Neither the state nor the church has been able to solve the problem of unity and diversity for the world as a whole. Both institutions establish premature unities which make it impossible to encompass further diversities constructively. Democratic states are especially successful in coordinating a variety of otherwise conflicting interests. But the best political organization still falls short of comprehensiveness, and sovereign nations constitute a new and often destructive source of diversity. Likewise, religious organizations, though dedicated to the peaceable redemption of the whole family of mankind, have in fact caused many bitter controversies and established deep and lasting cleavages.

In the light of these observations it is in order to suggest that the school may provide a basis for the creation of one human family, despite the multiplicity of interests, attitudes, and traditions. The community of scholarship, dedicated to the persistent search for truth, to investigation, discovery, and experimentation, is by its nature suited to the task of organizing the most diverse realities into some unity of experience.

Teachers and students, devoted unconditionally and fearlessly, to the full limits of their powers, to the total understanding of *what is* and *what is possible,* would appear to be in the best possible position to solve the ultimate problem of unity and diversity. The academic society thrives on differences. Variety sets problems for understanding and provides opportunity for widening of outlook. While schools exist and may function successfully in uniformist societies, in the long run the lifeblood of scholarship is the challenge of differences, demanding more ample perspectives and more penetrating insights.

Two decisively new features of modern culture in a period

of desperate need for human unity are the phenomenal proliferation of knowledge and the demand for universal education. The agencies of learning and teaching have become crucial in contemporary civilization. The accumulation and dissemination of information have become the hallmark of the age. Modern governments are not essentially different in kind from those of bygone eras. Religious organizations maintain their ancient traditions essentially unchanged. The manifold agencies of education, on the other hand, have so grown in scope and weight of responsibility that their function in the civilized world is genuinely new in kind. The task of creating a true family of man has now devolved primarily upon the institutions of education. If the school has received this commission it is because the fellowship of learners is in principle and by choice and conviction hospitable to pluralism. It is in essence an open society. The state and the church are significant and doubtless permanently useful ways of dealing with the problem of plurality, yet they are ever in danger of succeeding by destroying the differences they should serve to reconcile. The school, on the other hand, thrives on contrasts, because they provide the necessary stimulus for growth in competence and understanding.

These considerations point to the importance of the distinctions made earlier between intrinsically religious schools and schools with a derived religious basis. When the fundamental values and objectives of the school are derived from state or church, the limitations of those institutions with respect to comprehending differences are imported into the educational program. Hence the school is unable to make full use of its own power to advance further toward ultimacy. When the school is intrinsically religious, it becomes the privilege and duty of the learning community to put all things to the test, in order to discover what is indeed supremely important, best, most fundamental, inclusive, primordial, final, and meaningful, i.e., to be a fellowship of ultimate concern.

Schools which merely serve particular interests only accentuate the difficulties of coordinating individual and group differences. They become themselves part of the problem of pluralism. On the other hand, schools whose roots are sunk deeply into the very soil of the life of learning, schools whose foundations are in unlimited inquiry and in unconditional devotion to the truth, would seem to be singularly fitted to serve the harmonizing needs of a pluralistic civilization. From this standpoint it is of utmost importance that religious matters—questions of ultimate concern—not be assigned exclusively to organized religious bodies, but become the appropriate business also of the schools, including those not conducted by religious organizations. When fundamental questions concerning such problems as death and destiny, creation, and meaning arise in the course of the school experience, as they inevitably do, it does not serve the cause of education or of civilization well to turn the inquiry aside and to pass the responsibility back to church or family. Ultimate convictions condition the entire learning process, and cannot without great loss be relegated to a separate sphere of activity and institutional cultivation. The experiences of learning provide crucial occasions for generating ultimate concerns, and the school which through fear, ignorance, or indecisiveness refuses to deal responsibly with them fails in its central educational opportunity.

The intrinsically religious school is not the sole or even in every sense the primary social agency for the development of ultimate concern. Indeed, every domain of human experience provides occasions for religious insight. Learning in families, in the state, on the job, and at play—in any and every activity of life—may manifest ultimate concern. In particular, the historic religions may well afford exceptionally effective channels for ultimacy. The point being emphasized is that the school should be acknowledged as *one* important source of religious experience, in its own right, and not solely by derivation, and that the school is especially well suited as a context for the ultimate in pluralistic culture.

Religion and the school in American society

The problem of religion and the school is of historic and contemporary importance in American society. The miracle of America has been the creation of a unified commonwealth out of many different religious, racial, and national traditions. In ideal and actuality the nation has been characterized by its motto, *E pluribus unum*. One of the pillars upon which this achievement rests is the principle of separation of church and state, embodied in the First Amendment of the United States Constitution, which reads in part, "Congress shall make no laws respecting an establishment of religion, nor prohibiting the free exercise thereof."

This provision has permitted religions of many kinds to flourish, unhindered by state regulation. It has done justice to the freedom of the spirit, recognizing the priority of individual conscience and conviction. At the same time it has relieved government of ecclesiastical hindrances and obligations and of the insoluble problem of resolving theological differences. Both church and state have thriven on this demarcation of responsibilities, the one for the celebration and propagation of faith, the other for the regulation of civic life.

Just how complete the separation of church and state is, should be, or can be is a matter of continuing debate. Some advocate a high and impregnable wall of separation, others varying degrees of mutual support and cooperation short of establishment, i.e., official state sponsorship of organized religion. Since religious institutions own property and their members and officials engage in a variety of civic activities as representatives of those institutions, it seems evident that utter separation is impossible. Religious organizations as constituents of the body politic necessarily come within the purview of government. Thus in various ways both church and state exercise reciprocal influence over one another. The degrees, kinds, and limits of interrelationship are matters for continuing adjustment in custom and in law, and ultimately in the decisions of the courts culminating in the United States Supreme Court as highest interpreter of the Federal Constitution.

The principle of separation of church and state is so fundamental because in effect *it denies that ultimacy belongs by right either to the state or to the church.* A state with an established religion thereby sanctifies itself, and comes to be regarded as the temporal instrument of the divine will. An established religion is likewise confirmed in its exclusive claims when underwritten by the authority of the state. The limitation on both state and church implicit in the separation principle presupposes some other basis for ultimacy than these two institutions. The American people have had the wisdom not to enforce national unity through governmental suppression of freedom of belief and worship, and the historic fact of religious differences has made unity on the basis of a common religion impossible.

Upon what, then, has American social cohesion been established? The general answer would perhaps be: upon democratic ideals, such as equality, justice, and respect for the individual. Since these ideals have commonly been regarded as worthy of ultimate devotion, they have been essentially religious in character, and this status has often been symbolized by reference to the religious derivation and dedication of the national life in such phrases as "In God we trust" and "this nation under God." More concretely, the unifying ideals have been perpetuated through the educational system, especially the public schools. American universal free public education stands as evidence of the conviction that there is a common democratic heritage into which all the young should be inducted, and the success achieved in fashioning one people out of many diverse strands is due in large measure to these schools. Private education, too, has contributed to the richness and variety of American life, for the most part without threatening the fundamental ideals, and in many cases giving new vitality to them.

How has the principle of separation of church and state affected the schools? Its relevance stems from the fact that public schools are creations of the state, and as such must remain free of official connection with organized religion. Private schools may, of course, properly have such connections. As pointed out earlier, religion and church are not identical, and therefore it does not follow from the principle of separation of church and state that religion and public education must be separate. One of the crucial problems in American public education is the working out of its proper relationship to religion.

The continuing debate on religion in the public schools has generated two extreme positions, both of which seem clearly to err. At the one extreme are those who hold that the United States was founded on religious principles, that the great majority of the American people are committed to religion, and that the public schools ought therefore positively to teach belief in God, the Ten Commandments, and other central truths of the Judaeo–Christian heritage. The error of this way is that it seriously undermines the separation principle by giving governmental sanction and support to a particular theological and ecclesiastical tradition. It inescapably lends official authority to the historic theistic position as opposed to other religious outlooks which are symbolized in different ways.

At the other extreme are those who interpret the separation principle to mean that the public school should completely eliminate all religious elements from its program. Religion is a subject of endless and irresolvable dispute, say these spokesmen, and thus serves only to confuse and fragment public life, including that of the schools. The error of this way is that it impoverishes the school by excising from it an important aspect of actual human interest and experience. It also presupposes a narrow, purely traditional, and institutional conception of religion which precludes an examination of the basically religious foundations on which the public school program rests.

Both of these views depend upon the assumption that the religious element in education must be derived from sources outside the life of the school, e.g., from the churches or from the national tradition. A third position, which avoids the errors of both extremes, recognizes the religious foundations of the educative process itself. The school cannot be fully true to its own nature and task unless it seeks to ask and to propose answers to ultimate questions. In this perspective, the academic community ought not to remain on the level of the superficial and proximate, but should become aware of its own ultimate concerns. Such intrinsically religious schools do not violate the principle of separation of church and state. Indeed, they affirm and strengthen it, because they deny that churches have a monopoly of religion and demonstrate the possibility of cultivating faith without acknowledging the authority of any organized religion.

Organized religion is, however, by no means unimportant or irrelevant in these schools. Students and faculty bring with them into the academic setting a variety of institutional religious affiliations. The various organized religions are also significant facts of civilization. These realities of concrete religious life are data for consideration within the teaching–learning process. They provide important suggestions regarding ultimates. The essential point is that the traditional religious beliefs and practices are not simply imported and accepted on the authority of the parent religious institutions. They are rather taken as instrumentalities for the better exploration and expression of the deepest insights and commitments arising from within the authentic life of the school.

If the world of scholars and teachers is to provide the

depth and inclusiveness essential to the creation of a true family of mankind, despite contrasts of culture and conviction, the schools must learn to accept their own religious task. Such acceptance will establish the academic community in responsibility and maturity without in the least infringing the principle of church–state separation. In fact, it will give the schools the authority to lead and the freedom to co-operate with the state and organized religion in the making of a human commonwealth transcending the rivalries of nations and sects.

3 RELIGION AND THE TEACHER

THE quality of school experience is to a large degree determined by the teacher. Hence, in considering the religious foundations of education it is necessary to examine the religious aspects of the teacher's work.

Personal life witness

The first and perhaps most crucial way in which religion enters into teaching is in the witness which the teacher makes through his personal life. The total being of the teacher inevitably creates an impression on students and associates. By his general outlook and bearing he radiates around himself a field of influence. In a host of ways, often subtle and for the most part unintended, he communicates to those about him the nature of his personal faith. The religious situation of any person is defined by what he most truly loves, i.e., by what concerns him ultimately. The teacher makes his object of worship known by every indication of what most deeply interests him, of how he measures his successes and failures, of the sources from which he seeks strength and solace, and of his criteria of choice in making important decisions. What counts in the living witness is not primarily an explicit rational system of belief but the implicit values and commitments which govern the actual organization of the person's life.

The teacher cannot avoid communicating his own religion in this fundamental sense. What he *is* will more surely and impressively be taught than anything he says. Students will learn what the teacher's life really means by observing what he puts his trust in, what are the grounds for his confidence, and the objects of his fear, affection, and reverence. Teachers who are devoted to mean and petty things teach a degraded and degrading faith. Those who worship the intellect teach the religion of reason. Those for whom mankind is the supreme good bear witness to a humanistic religion. Teachers dedicated to a religious institution communicate an ecclesiastical faith. Those who believe in the supremacy of love and the need and power of forgiveness and reconciliation teach a religion of compassion and redemption.

It is therefore not necessarily a commendation to affirm that by the witness of his life a teacher advertises his faith. The religion thus announced may be immature or mature, founded upon error or upon truth, debased or exalted. The responsibility of teachers is unavoidable and weighty. Since they do exercise influence on students, often decisive, it is incumbent upon all who undertake the office of instruction to look carefully to their own faith, not imagining that the light by which they are guided can remain hidden behind the shield of formal professional activities. The teacher who seriously considers the faith by which he lives and which he therefore teaches can hardly avoid the question whether he should really want his students to live by the same affections and to the same ends.

The communication of faith by personal life witness presupposes that the teacher has achieved some reasonably coherent personal character, that his life is organized according to a consistent pattern of values with some clear distinction between the more and the less valuable. If he is tossed about by the shifting currents of experience, merely responsive to local and momentary influences, if he is without abiding convictions by which to direct his life, he can bear no clear and unmistakable witness. To teach effectively by one's life requires a certain wholeness of personality, an integrity and centeredness of being. To lack this is to be without faith, and thus to be subject to determination by chance circumstance rather than by authentic personal commitments.

Teaching by personal life witness obviously occurs in all types of schools. The teacher in a church school communicates his faith in this way no more than one who teaches in a public school. No law, no wall of separation of church and state, can intercept the unspoken message of faith which radiates to the pupil from the teacher's life. Perhaps the witness is often even more effective in a non-church school than in a church school, since in an officially religious school the teacher may be cast in a stereotyped churchly role which tends to obscure his real faith.

Interpersonal life witness

The teacher bears witness to his faith not only by the evidence of what he is in himself, but also by his manner of relating to his students. The latter way cannot, of course, be sharply distinguished from the former, since the very being of a person is in part a product of his interactions with other persons, and since the test of what a person *is* is what he *does,* particularly in relation to others. It is by one's fruits, chiefly in interpersonal conduct, that he is known. Nevertheless, it is useful to make a distinction between the teaching of faith through being oneself, in whatever ways that may be manifest in the various activities of life, and teaching specifically through conduct with respect to students.

Here the primary question is whether or not the teacher regards his students as important and valuable. Do they enter, as persons, into his ultimate concern, or is his orientation such as to make them incidental to making a living, gaining intellectual prestige, or conducting research? For some teachers, pupils are important, but have negative value; they are a source of irritation, they are hindrances in the path of satisfaction and professional achievement.

Teaching is fundamentally religious only when the teacher–student relationship falls within the compass of the teacher's supreme interest and dedication. The manner of interaction must also be more than routine, casual, or arbitrary. It should not rest upon superficial appearances, but upon the most reliable available knowledge and the deepest intuitions regarding human personality and its nurture. The profoundly religious teacher does not regard his students in the manner of a hotel keeper, as transients to be cared for while they are assigned to his class, without regard to their origins or destinations. Instead, he makes it his business to understand each person as fully and sympathetically as possible, in the light of past influences and of hopes, expectations, and possibilities for the future. Such a teacher tries to relate to each pupil as a whole and enduring person, and not as a passing feature of the job environment.

The crucial difference between an ultimate interpersonal life witness and one which falls short of this goal is that in the former the teacher treats other persons as persons—as unique subjects, each capable of apprehending and participating in boundless possibilities—while in the latter others are regarded more as objects. *Things* can be manipulated; *persons* as such must be dealt with as free and responsible agents. Civilized communities claim for the most part to have abolished the cruel and outrageous practice of human sacrifice, yet it must be asked whether every occasion—and there are countless such occasions in the most advanced modern societies—when human beings are treated as objects is not simply a different and more subtle form of the same barbarity. In particular, it may be suggested that anyone who, even for the highest of motives, teaches as though students were things rather than free, creative persons in effect engages in human sacrifice, i.e., in the act of offering up the life of another on the altar of pedagogical fashion, expediency, or abstract ideal.

Truly ultimate concern drives the teacher beyond the confines of his own egocentricity toward genuine caring for others. As long as students are regarded as objects, they can be arranged within the pattern of the teacher's own scheme of life. The religious outlook requires a transcending of every finite and self-satisfied pattern, and the acknowledgment that one's ego is not in truth the source and center of all being and meaning. Freedom from this illusion is gained chiefly through recognizing and respecting other persons as important and worthful in their own right and not only as they conform to and confirm one's own ego. Hence the quality of interpersonal relationships is a basic aspect of the religious significance of the teacher's work.

Witness by word

The teacher has no choice but to communicate his faith through his personal life and his interpersonal relationships. These are mute but nonetheless eloquent witnesses to his governing commitments. But the teacher may also express his faith in words. He may seek to explain more fully who he is and why he behaves as he does toward others by offering a verbal interpretation of his life and conduct. In this way the life witness is made conscious and articulate.

The value of such verbal expression of faith is its economy and efficiency. By the use of word symbols an abundance of meaning can be transmitted quickly and often with clarity and precision. Furthermore, by confessing his faith a teacher can supplement, confirm, and intensify the witness which he makes in being and act. If he makes traditional statements of faith such as "I believe in God," "I trust in Jesus Christ," or "I worship the God of Israel and keep His law," the teacher also taps the reservoirs of meaning contained in time-honored formulae.

Unfortunately the witness by word easily falls into irrelevance or hypocrisy. The words may not agree with the life which they purport to express, in which case they degenerate into mere talk. The one who utters them may be unconscious of the lack of correspondence between what he says and what he is and does, yet the effect on those with whom he associates is much the same as if he deliberately misrepresented his convictions. Verbal formulae are so much less costly than true loving and right living that one is constantly tempted to substitute the former for the latter. This is especially true of teachers, one of whose chief professional skills is talking. Words can be so swiftly uttered and so easily arranged according to the accepted models of perfection that those who are expert in using them may easily come to regard them as the very substance of faith.

Verbal witness may thus tend to confirm the view that religion consists simply of a set of ideas or propositions to which one gives assent. Faith comes to be regarded as belief in certain truths, which are frequently accepted on the authority of the one who teaches them. In this way the ultimate concern which is the inner substance of religion and which the words should symbolize is lost from view, the superficial and external forms are mistaken for the living reality, and religion is rendered formal, conventional, and trivial.

Even when an attempt is made to penetrate to the life meanings behind the words, the difficulty arises that most statements of traditional religious belief are both vague and ambiguous. Such a simple, basic affirmation as "I believe in God," even if understood in any definable sense, as it usually is not, means different things to different people and is interpreted variously in the several religious traditions. Hence the teacher who witnesses to his faith by word may have on his hands a difficult problem of interpreting his meaning, especially if the students come from a variety of religious backgrounds. A life witness, on the other hand, is less ambiguous. Because of this, the teacher's being and doing are a crucial religious influence in the school, and also provide the best means of explicating the verbal confession of faith.

For the reasons suggested above, the witness by word should be employed with considerable caution and circumspection. The teacher should confess his faith only when he is convinced by deep heart-searching that the language truly represents his ultimate concerns and then only in situations where the students are able to understand the words with reasonable clarity and where they actually need and desire the word witness to confirm and illuminate the life witness. The circumstances are less likely to be appropriate in a public school, with the usual diversity of religious backgrounds of the students and in view of the principle of separation of church and state, than in a private school, particularly one under church auspices. Word witness is also generally less appropriate in teaching younger children than at the older ages, since the former are less able to understand and criticize verbal abstractions. Yet even in the public schools and even with young children the teacher need not feel that his lips are sealed against any utterance about his religious faith. His real convictions can hardly remain hidden in any case, and students are usually also aware of his formal religious affiliations, if any. Therefore it would be pointless for the teacher not to feel free, on occasion, to tell what he believes.

Teaching religion

Teaching becomes religious in an explicit and formal sense when instruction is given in the tenets of one of the organized faiths, when these beliefs are represented as the true ones, and when the students are expected to accept them as such. This goes far beyond teaching by bearing witness to one's own faith, either by one's life or by word. The teacher generally cannot and should not hide his personal commitments. But it is a different matter when the teacher assumes the task of inculcating a system of religious belief and practice in the students.

Instruction in a traditional religion is appropriate in a school operated under the auspices of an organized religious group. A major purpose of such a private school is usually to propagate the faith, and this can frequently be accomplished by formal religious instruction. Doctrinal teaching of this sort may also be given in public schools when there is an officially recognized or established religion. But in the United States, where the nation is committed to a policy of separation and impartiality with respect to organized religion, sectarian religious instruction is inadmissible.

Still, even in the case of the public schools, it is a question whether religious teaching of every sort can and should be excluded. It is easy enough to identify and eliminate actual doctrinal teaching, as, for example, of Christianity or Judaism. It is not so evident that the teaching of other less traditionally religious systems of belief can be avoided. The teacher not only has a faith of his own and for himself, but he also must have certain convictions which are fundamental to his teaching and which he consciously or unconsciously seeks to have his students accept. It is these most basic values, such as loyalty to the truth, willingness to modify established beliefs in the light of new evidence, and regard for individual worth, personal freedom, and responsibility, which the teacher feels obliged to implant in his students without any sense of violating the principles of religious freedom and church–state separation. In fact, these principles may be integral to the very faith which the teacher seeks to transmit.

From this vantage point, in every school, private or public, religion in the sense of ultimate concern may and must be taught. Teaching of religion in the conventional sense of traditional doctrine can be avoided in the public schools, but the more fundamental inculcation of governing convictions is an intrinsic feature of the educative process. It is accordingly of importance that the teacher become aware of the supreme values to which his teaching is in fact dedicated and that every possible resource for the constructive criticism and improvement of these ultimate beliefs be utilized.

Teaching about religion

Instead of teaching religion the teacher may teach *about* religion. By this is meant a factual, intellectual, objective treatment of the subject of religion. The teacher in this approach does not recommend a faith to the students for acceptance. He merely helps them to understand the facts about religion as one significant component of the culture of mankind. Individuals and groups do have religious beliefs, engage in religious activities, and establish religious institutions. It would seem feasible to teach these facts, dispassionately and without personal involvement, just as one would teach about economic systems, marriage customs, or political parties.

This teaching about religion is not, however, as simple and straightforward as it first appears. The difficulty lies in judging what the facts really are, which are the important ones, and what they mean. "Bare facts" do not exist. Every fact must be expressed in some conceptual framework, which presupposes an interpretive scheme. The "real truth" about religion or anything else depends upon the criteria of reality and truth employed. To be sure, there are facts such as religious census data on which everyone can agree. But convictions about the importance and implications of these data differ. For example, there would be little even preliminary agreement concerning the Protestant Reformation or the Crusades among those of the Protestant, Roman Catholic, and Muslim faiths.

It also can be argued that a religion looks different from

outside the faith than from within, so that an objective discussion of "facts," even so far as this is possible, is never a treatment of the religion itself. According to this view, to present the externals of a religion is not to represent it in any sense as it truly is; one can only know it and communicate it from within.

There is the related practical objection to the so-called objective teaching about religion that parents and clergy may object strongly to having anyone outside the religious community itself give instruction in their faith, regardless of how factual the teaching is intended to be. Jewish parents do not want Christian teachers explaining Judaism to their children, Christian parents equally reject a Jewish teacher's handling of Christianity, and parents in both groups object to having their religion explained by one without any religious affiliation.

To these critical problems should be added the further one that few teachers have the requisite knowledge to deal with the facts of organized religion fairly and intelligently. The variations and intricacies of creed and rite are so great and the questions of interpretation so complex and confusing that it may seem appropriate only for those who have specialized in religious studies to try to teach about religion.

These difficulties with factual religious teaching are likely to be more serious in a public school, with different religious affiliations represented by the students and with policy controlled by a pluralist citizenry, than in a private school, and more especially in a church school, with a more uniform student population and policy-making constituency.

In spite of the difficulties, a strong case can still be made for teaching about religion, even in public schools. The most obvious point in its favor is the patent obligation of the teacher to do maximum justice to all important realities of culture. Religion has played a significant part—sometimes for good and at other times for ill—in civilization. The well-educated person may not remain in ignorance of these facts of civilization. Granted the complexity of religious history and thought, there is no excuse for not attempting a fair and balanced treatment of these topics. Other subjects, such as modern scientific discoveries and political or economic theories, are also difficult, frequently controversial, and susceptible of varying interpretations, yet they are ingredients in the cultural heritage, and few would deny the possibility and desirability of teaching about them.

The objection that a religion cannot be fairly presented by one outside the faith is also not decisive. The essence of human intelligence is to be able to transcend one's own individual standpoint and by the power of sympathetic imagination to enter the world of thought and feeling of other people. A good teacher has this capacity to an unusual degree. He can present various points of view to his students as vividly and persuasively as if they were his own. He may thus actually have the awareness and perspective which enable him to do better justice to these points of view than would be done by most insiders. Moreover, a good teacher also expects his students to read and to discuss, in this way affording greater balance, proportion, and independent judgment about the religions studied. As for the further objection that church members resent having their faith presented by teachers who do not share their beliefs, this is a practical political problem which must be met with tact, patience, and understanding, but also with the firm conviction that the teacher has a professional responsibility to present the truth as he sees it and that no group has the right or authority to reserve any domain of human experience as its own exclusive concern.

Leadership in ritual acts

Another approach to religious teaching is the conducting of ritual acts, such as reading from the Bible, giving public prayers, singing hymns, and celebrating religious festivals.

Activities of this kind are designed as corporate symbolic expressions of faith. They are communal celebrations of religious dedication. As such, they presuppose a common commitment among those who participate. It follows that the practice of corporate devotions is not appropriate in a school where the students have differing religious loyalties. Furthermore, acts of worship reflect the practice of organized religious communities and hence are not proper within the American public schools, in view of the Constitutional principle of church–state separation.

Notwithstanding the evident inappropriateness of these practices, many teachers continue to engage in them. Not only so, but the laws of some states explicitly permit or even require certain ritual acts in the public schools, such as daily reading from the Bible or repetition of the Lord's Prayer. In what would seem to be a violation of the spirit of the Constitution in matters religious, the Congress of the United States has also seen fit to adopt an explicit theological formula ("In God we trust") as the national motto, and to insert into the pledge of allegiance to the flag, regularly recited in public schools, the theological phrase "one nation, under God." As reflections of majority belief such expressions are doubtless justified. But as statements of official religious sanction they are inadmissible, since they cast a shadow on the loyalty and acceptability of the many citizens who do not share these theistic beliefs. In view of these legislative developments it is natural that many teachers, especially those with formal religious affiliations, feel justified in leading their students in ritual acts.

Providing occasions for traditional forms of corporate devotion is in reality the most explicit and direct way of teaching religion. In these acts the teacher does not simply bear witness to his own faith or recommend the acceptance of certain beliefs; he tacitly assumes that the students are already committed to a specific faith and he asks them to make overt profession of their devotions as, for example, in prayers, pledges, and hymns. The lesson is reinforced by the conformity of the other students; it is difficult for a solitary objector to withstand the social pressure.

Such religious devotions in the public school not only violate American principles of freedom of worship, but also are religiously and educationally detrimental. They frequently engender a routine and perfunctory attitude toward religious practice, and encourage the view that religion is a specialized activity which can be taken care of in five or ten minutes of morning "exercises" and then be put out of mind until the next day. Usually no attempt is made to relate the acts of worship to the other activities of the school. This is illustrated in the practice (in some states under legislative stipulation) of reading from the Bible *without comment.* The prohibition of comment is designed, of course, to prevent teachers from interpreting the scripture according to their own sectarian biases. What the students actually learn, however, is that the Bible is the one book one dare not talk about, and therefore need not think about. In short, the Bible is made educationally irrelevant.

There is a way of using ritual acts which overcomes the foregoing objections. They may be employed as demonstrations of how various religious groups worship. All students are then not expected to participate in the activities, but only those who wish to do so, either as committed to the faith being celebrated or as actors playing a role. For example, a selected group may sing Christmas hymns as a demonstration of how Christians celebrate the birth of Christ. This is a different matter from asking an entire class comprised of Christians, Jews, and those with no religious affiliation, to join in such a hymn as "Joy to the World." Similarly, it is reasonable to ask a class to listen respectfully to the offering of prayers in one or more traditions, but not to expect a public school class as part of its state-sanctioned instruction to repeat together the Lord's (Jesus Christ's) Prayer. Since the use of ritual acts for purposes of demonstration is in reality a further way of teaching *about* religion, the comments made in the preceding section are applicable also to this type of religious teaching. Instead of engendering a view of religion as routine and irrelevant, this approach tends to encourage discussion, reflection, and application to other areas of educational concern.

The major importance of ritual acts in teaching lies in their power to express ultimate concerns vividly and concretely. Religion which is contained simply in the verbal formulas of literal factual discourse can scarcely appeal to the whole person with emotion and will as well as intellect. In a church school the faith of the sponsoring religious organization can be celebrated by appropriate traditional rites in which the students participate as members of the community of believers. In a public school traditional ritual acts may be used to portray by objective demonstration the nature of organized religion as a fact of culture. There are also modes of celebration peculiar to academic institutions, such as commencement or commemoration ceremonies, not derived from the organized religious tradition but nonetheless fundamentally religious in character, which are suitable for participation by all students, and expressive of the deepest commitments binding together members of the community of learning.

The teacher's commitment

Every aspect of the teacher's work is, as we have seen, governed by his ultimate concerns. The teacher cannot remain neutral and uncommitted. He cannot teach without making decisions about methods, programs, and objectives. These decisions reveal what the teacher believes to be of most importance, supremely valuable, and chiefly to be avoided. They express the teacher's faith.

Faith there must be. The crucial question is, Faith in what? How adequate is that to which the teacher is committed? How worthy of devotion is that upon which his life is based? Is his object of dedication partial or comprehensive, superficial or profound, unrelated or meaningful, derived or original, preliminary or final? In other words, is the commitment truly an ultimate one?

Like everyone else, teachers are reluctant to accept the responsibilities of commitment. But to an unusual degree the teacher is subject to the illusion that he can escape this burden of his freedom. Academic people are prone to regard themselves as somehow above the strife of values competing for allegiance, as inhabitants of a region of pure, untroubled objectivity in which all possibilities forever lie open for contemplation. It is true that a special function of the teacher is that of imaginative exploration of alternatives, but this by no means contradicts the truth that even teachers cannot remain totally uncommitted. It is simply that for the teacher the scope and complexity of ingredients for choice are greater than for many other callings. Moreover, the stakes are especially high in the case of the teacher's commitment, because his loyalties are not only relevant to himself; they also directly, and often decisively, influence those whom he teaches.

Teaching for commitment

Teaching thus has religious foundations in the teacher's ultimate concerns, which are reflected in his life and words, in his teaching of religion (in the traditional sense) or his teaching about it, and in his leadership in ritual acts. Yet none of these religious aspects of teaching is in the most fundamental sense religious teaching. Basic religion is taught when the student is led to make his own ultimate commitments. The really crucial requirement for the teacher is not that he communicate his own beliefs—though this is important and inevitable—but that he assist the student to become a person in his own right, with values and convictions which truly belong to him.

Teaching is the nurture of personal growth. It is the provision of means for the development of mature, whole human beings. Such complete persons have within themselves a center and source of being, a principle of evaluation and decision, a pattern of self-determination. Hence the teacher ought always to provide a basis and opportunities for the student to make responsible decisions and thus to discover and determine himself. It is not the teacher's faith which the student needs; rather, his need is for a faith of his own. The religious foundation of teaching is not in the propagation of the teacher's ultimate commitments to the growing person but in the encouragement of uniquely personal patterns of dedication in the student. To this end the teacher should not urge upon the pupil the adoption of an official faith, but should in season and out help him to grow in the life of faith appropriate to his own nature.

Further consideration of how personal loyalties are formed makes it clear, however, that no sharp division may be drawn between the adoption of others' commitments and the appropriation of a faith for oneself. A person usually comes to count as his own the values which are most precious to the parents and teachers who have influenced him in his childhood. Moreover, it would obviously be absurd to suggest that a young child be urged to make responsible decisions about what is most important and valuable for his life. Teachers of children must affirm certain values and assume that for the most part they will be accepted. The dependent child must develop largely within the context of decisions governed by the concerns and commitments of his elders. The teacher cannot simply present a youngster with a range of possibilities and urge him to make up his own mind. On what basis is the choice to be made? Is the impulse of the moment, to which the immature chiefly respond, a suitable criterion? Must not some standard of worth more ultimate in reference be applied externally until such time as the learner can grasp it as his own?

Personal commitment to valuable ends in maturity depends upon a secure and consistent structure of existence in the early years of life, together with a gradual extension of the domain of free and responsible choice. Personality cannot develop properly if alternatives are left open at every stage, without firm guidance by the more mature. But neither should the teacher affirm his way to be ultimately true and right and expect the student always to adopt it obediently and unquestioningly.

Teaching for commitment is a fundamental objective of every stage of personal growth, but the methods of practicing it must be different for the younger and the older student. Childhood should establish a *basis* for freedom, youth and adulthood should give opportunity for exercising it. Generally one's own mature loyalties will turn out to be the same as the faith of the fathers. Freedom does not require rejection of what has been built into one by society and culture. What it does demand is personal exploration, examination, and acceptance of the old, or the new, as the root and ground of one's being.

In both private and public schools it is the religious obligation of the teacher to lay upon each student the importance of giving heart and mind to the faith by which he lives. It is not the teacher's task to dictate with authority the commitments to be adopted. Rather, he should teach with the consciousness that through all he does he wants the student to grow into a meaningful personal relationship to that which is most worthy of his freely given devotion.

Teaching and creation

Teaching is an act of creation and thus falls within that aspect of religion concerned with beginnings. The teacher participates in a making of persons. This is surely a task to be approached with the humility, awe, and reverence characteristic of religious devotion. It is a sacred responsibility to have a hand in fashioning human personalities, the highest of all the orders of created beings. Linked with creation is also destiny, for upon the manner of the teacher's creating depends the future of mankind. Those into whom the teacher today helps breathe the breath of life will be the mature members of tomorrow's society, who will determine its character and tendencies.

As a creator of men and society the teacher engages in the work proper to God himself. In this position the teacher is tempted to usurp the place of the divine and to seek to fashion his students according to his own pattern and will, or, even more likely, in the image of himself. That is, he assumes full and complete authority for directing and controlling the lives of the growing persons committed to his care. To do so is, of course, the height of pretension and an act of sacrilege.

How can the teacher resist the temptation to play God? To renounce all responsibility for guiding human growth is not the answer. That would mean in fact giving up teaching. It is not necessary to choose between irresponsibility and usurpation of divine authority. One may teach with strength and conviction without playing God, under three conditions: First, the teacher must acknowledge that such insight and virtue as he possesses are ultimately not of his own making but are gifts to him from the primal sources of wisdom and goodness. These gifts he is privileged to employ, as an agent of the divine, for the like benefit of others. Second, the teacher must be aware of the distortion which he as a finite and self-justifying creature inevitably imposes upon the best gifts of intelligence and affection bestowed upon him. Hence he may not ascribe perfection or final authority to any conviction, no matter how firmly he is persuaded of its rightness. In the third place, the teacher must recognize the operation of creative powers within the student himself, so that the nurture of persons is not conceived as the work of a human craftsman who fashions a product out of passive stuff, but as a constructive interweaving of distinct and unique centers of creative activity.

Teaching is indeed a religious enterprise in respect to its creative quality. The teacher and the student both belong to a web of existence in which lives are being made. In this process each has a different role to play. The teacher is not God, but he does have the opportunity of sharing to an unusual degree in the making of persons.

Teaching as a ministry

The work of the teacher may be regarded as a kind of sacred ministry. Like the priest at the altar, the teacher is charged with providing channels through which life, light, and strength may come to those whom he serves. He is a steward of truth, which, like the holy mysteries of the temple, must be mediated by finite symbols that hide as well as reveal their fathomless referent. The teacher also has an evangel to proclaim: the good news of freedom and fulfillment through true knowledge and right conduct. He points out ways which lead from frustration and weakness to fruition and power.

As a minister, the teacher regards himself as a representative of what is ultimately true and good. He does not assert his own primacy and authority, as if he were the incarnation of perfection. Instead, he seeks to make himself an effective vehicle for the truth, and he sees his task as one of mediation between his students and "the most high." Wherein lies the essential distinction between teaching which has genuinely religious foundations (i.e., a basis in that which is really ultimate) and teaching which has no such basis? In the latter case the teacher endeavors simply to satisfy the particular demands of himself, his students, or society; he is content to exercise certain well-defined specialized functions. In religious teaching the reference transcends all such limited concerns, and the teacher dedicates each act to the service of that supreme righteousness and truth which is forever beyond but never irrelevant to all concrete realizations. This is the difference between teaching as a technical activity and teaching as a ministry.

The vocation of teaching

In the religious tradition it is customary to speak of a special vocation to the ministry. Everyone is regarded as having some distinct work to do in the service of God, but the idea of a "calling" is especially pertinent to holy orders. One may enter many occupations simply on the basis of personal interest, special skill and aptitude, social need, or accidents of circumstance. With the ministry it is different; one should enter it—so the conviction goes—only if he has had a definite and unmistakable commission from the divine.

While there are obvious psychological and theological shortcomings in a literal doctrine of special vocation, it does seem important to emphasize the exceptional religious potentiality of certain occupations. Teaching, like the sacred ministry, is one of these. Teaching ought to be regarded not merely as a job but as a calling. In many kinds of work it does not make much objective difference whether or not the task is done with a sense of ultimate concern. In teaching it does make a decisive difference, for in the guidance of human growth it is the whole pattern of the teacher's basic convictions which is of most influence on the students. In the performance of his functions the teacher's entire being is involved, and he in turn affects the whole personalities of his students.

When the teacher regards his work as a vocation, he possesses a sense of *mission.* His teaching has direction, purpose, and meaning. He is animated by a consciousness of high goals to be achieved. He is glad to have been chosen to play a part in a great divine–human drama of creating persons. Teaching is thus not simply a work selected for convenience or for personal satisfaction, but a willing self-dedication to the faithful discharge of solemn yet joyful responsibilities.

4 RELIGION AND THE CURRICULUM

BROADLY conceived, the school curriculum is the entire program of study and learning planned for the students. It includes not only specific formal courses and the procedures used to teach them but also out-of-class activities designed to promote the students' development.

The present chapter considers the place of religion in the curriculum. Much of what has been said in the preceding chapters on the school and on the teacher has unavoidably trespassed on the topic of religion in the curriculum. The nature and functions of schools and of teaching can only by arbitrary abstraction be distinguished from curricular concerns.

In what follows we shall discuss the main possible ways in which religion may be manifest in the curriculum. In making this analysis it will be necessary to utilize the distinction developed in Chapter 1 between formal, organized, traditional religion and religion as ultimate concern. Obviously the place of religion in the curriculum, especially in public schools, depends upon which conception of religion is understood.

Required courses in religion

Certain formal courses of study in religion may be offered and required of all students. If religion really has to do with matters of ultimate concern, it would seem to follow that no subject of study is more important than religion and that courses in religion ought to be the one essential and universal ingredient of the curriculum. No student should be considered well educated unless he has acquired right beliefs about what is of supreme importance and of highest value, since it is these convictions which govern every activity of life.

Schools conducted under the auspices of organized religion usually do include religious studies as a part of the required curriculum, and some schools in which the centrality of religion is taken with full seriousness include such sacred studies at every stage and level of the curriculum. Religion, it is said, is not a subject one can learn once and for all and then move on to other topics. It is the very heart and soul of every student's program, giving meaning, unity, and vitality to all of the other subjects. Perennial in interest and relevance, and inexhaustibly rich in possibilities for exploration and insight, it is the one indispensable curricular offering.

In some officially religious schools, however, the religion requirement is more modest. It may be considered sufficient for the student to take a single course or a few basic courses in religion, in order to give him an understanding of the fundamentals of the faith. It may also be considered that the formal study of religion need not begin until a specified level of maturity or, on the other hand, that it need not continue beyond a particular age. In some schools religious studies may be required of students in the liberal arts but not in the technical divisions, on the assumption that religion, like history and philosophy, is one of the humane disciplines. All such limitations of the requirements for sacred studies give evidence of a specialized conventional view of religion rather than one of ultimate concern.

In countries with an established religion, schools conducted by the state may be expected to require the study of the official religion, though in some cases with exemptions for students with a different private religious affiliation. In the United States, where state sponsorship of sectarian religion is forbidden by law, required courses in the tenets of one organized religion would certainly have no place in public schools. It would be argued by some, however, that even in public education, particularly at the higher levels, it might be both legal and desirable to require of all students some study, under teachers of competence, broad sympathies, and scholarly objectivity, of religious problems and of the major living faiths.

When courses in religion are required, a decision must be reached about the nature of the study materials to be used. The most common resource has been the sacred scriptures. Scripture study is standard in Jewish and in Protestant Christian schools, as well as in the education of Muslims, Buddhists, and Hindus. Roman Catholics give priority to instruction in the doctrines of the Church, which have their basis in scripture and tradition. Besides courses in Bible and in doctrine, the program of religious study may include the history of religions or of a particular religious tradition, the comparative analysis of the religions of mankind, the reading of religious classics, a religious approach to ethical issues, or a consideration of basic intellectual and practical problems in the field of religion. The choice of materials most appropriate for the religion courses depends upon many factors, including the general religious orientation of the school, the religious backgrounds of the students, their emotional and intellectual maturity, and the amount of time available for instruction in religion.

Apart from any applicable legal restrictions, there are two principal objections to required courses in religion. The first is that the ultimate concern which may motivate the establishment of obligatory religious studies is frequently not communicated to the students through the requirement. Since the religion courses are usually regarded simply as particular units of work to be completed, like all other courses, the ultimacy is lost sight of and religion becomes merely one special interest among others. The obligatory character of the requirement tends to obscure the element of free wholehearted personal response which is essential to genuine faith, and to make of religion a duty which can be mechanically discharged.

Closely related to this objection is a second one, that having a religion requirement in the curriculum may tend to make other parts of the curriculum religiously sterile. If it is assumed that religion can be taken care of in designated religion courses, responsibility will not be felt for taking account of religious facts and dimensions in other areas of study.

Elective courses in religion

Instead of requiring students to take courses in religion, an elective option may be provided. This method has the advantages of dissociating the study of religion from compulsion and of securing for the courses the sincere interest which is evident in the free decision to elect them. While this inner motivation is helpful in any course of study, it is most important in the study of religion, which rests upon an act of personal commitment. That is to say, the meaningfulness and effectiveness of the course are enhanced if the purposes of the students taking it agree with rather than contradict the spirit of the subject studied.

The major disadvantage of putting the study of religion on an elective basis is that it reinforces the view of religion as a specialized and optional human pursuit—a domain of thought and action available for those who have a taste for it but by no means essential to every person. Some people (so runs the implied argument) are interested in sports or world affairs, other people in religion; each has his own personal preoccupations, and religion may be one of these; as one of the many interests of mankind, opportunity should be provided for the formal study of religion; some students will elect it out of a special sense of need for solace or assurance, others will choose it because of their special aptitudes for religious experience or because they find it intellectually interesting; for many religion is an enjoyable hobby, for a a few it provides an occupation.

An elective approach to religion is, of course, contrary to the understanding of religion as ultimate concern. The objection is not decisive, because religion is not the same as the formal study of religion and therefore there is no *necessary* contradiction between being fundamentally religious and taking or offering elective courses in religion. The point is that a curricular arrangement in which religion is offered as one specialized department of study among others like accounting, esthetics, and American history suggests and confirms a conventional and less-than-ultimate conception of religion.

Elective courses in religion have been suggested as an appropriate solution to the problem of teaching religion in the American public schools. If the courses are freely elected, no one can claim that freedom of religion is violated. Furthermore, it is even possible to teach religion according to the several organized traditions, students being divided into classes according to denominational preference or affiliation. Opponents of this system object to its divisiveness. They emphasize the function of the public schools as a unifying factor in American democracy and they deplore the fragmentation of the public school community into denominational groups for the study of religion.

Sectarian religious teaching, even on an elective basis, has also been attacked as a violation of the American principle of separation of church and state. Furthermore, some children may not elect to study religion at all, and when the great majority do so elect, the few dissenting children are seemingly put under psychological pressure and at a disadvantage in comparison with the others.

The debate over elective courses in religion has centered chiefly around the program of *released time* study of religion. Under this program the public school releases students during part of the regular school hours for attendance at separate religion classes conducted under the auspices of the various organized religious groups. Through two important decisions (*McCollum v. Board of Education,* 1948, and *Zorach v. Clauson,* 1952) the United States Supreme Court has affirmed the constitutionality of released time instruction, provided the classes are not conducted on public school property. This position of the highest American court on released time confirms the view that opposition of church and state is not implied by the doctrine of separation in the First Amendment, for in such programs the state lends indirect support to sectarian religious instruction, though without showing any preference for one denomination over another and without compelling anyone to attend religious classes.

Apart from the legal question, the released time program is susceptible to the tendency of all elective studies to become specialized and unrelated activities. The fact of dividing the students into separate denominational groups and taking them away from the school for religious classes dramatizes the particularistic character of religion. It must therefore be asked whether the hour or two per week gained for church instruction is not bought at the expense of integral, relevant, and truly ultimate religious understanding.

Religion as incidental to other courses

Religion may enter the curriculum through courses in traditional academic subject fields, or as a component of studies organized around problems and interests, rather than in courses in religion as such. This approach was discussed in the immediately preceding chapter from the standpoint of the teacher, as "teaching about religion." In the present chapter we consider the same approach from the somewhat different perspective of curriculum construction.

The case for including the facts about religious belief and practice in all their major forms, as part of the material of instruction, to be introduced when and as necessary for the understanding of the cultural heritage, would seem to be irrefutable. No educator can in good conscience and with professional integrity counsel that such a pervasive and influential human phenomenon as religion be ignored in the school curriculum.

At the same time the presentation of information about religion in the various courses should not become a cloak for defending or attacking particular religious views. Since religion is rightly conceived as a matter of conviction and not of pure dispassionate intellect, it is natural to feel that the consideration of religion will tend to be persuasive in character. But this is not necessarily the case. It is possible to expound facts and issues with clarity and insight without partisanship, recognizing differences of interpretation and belief and not presuming full possession of ultimate truth despite the fervency of one's own convictions. Information concerning religious history, beliefs, organization, ethical codes, and cultic practice can be presented by well-informed teachers in connection with the study of literature, philosophy, history, social and natural sciences, and the arts just as intelligently and fairly as any other matters of abiding human interest. That any subject, including religion, is controversial, deeply involved with emotion, and susceptible of widely differing interpretations is no reason for excluding it from the curriculum. On the contrary, it is just these real issues which give life and zest to any course of study.

The presentation of religion in connection with other

courses should always be governed by the principle of genuine relevance to the subject under consideration. It is contrary to good scholarship and to educational integrity to look for pretexts to introduce religious ideas. For example, frequent and fervent references to the majesty and power of God manifest in the creation, however right and sincere in themselves, do not contribute directly to progress in the study of astronomy. For the most part theological considerations are irrelevant to this subject. In the study of American history in colonial times, on the other hand, knowledge of religious beliefs and movements is essential. But even here, the references to religion might be improperly employed as an occasion for basically irrelevant religious or anti-religious commentary and not for the purpose of advancing the study at hand.

The advantage in including religion throughout the curriculum is that the relevance of religion to the whole of existence is thereby acknowledged and the sense of ultimacy tends to be preserved. On the other hand, the treatment of religion as incidental to other courses may fail to do full justice to the inner meaning of religion by giving attention chiefly to it as an objective cultural phenomenon. This approach suggests a less than ultimate view, in treating religion simply as one of many factors in the social process, coordinate (for example) with economic, political, and emotional influences.

The objective incidental treatment of religion throughout the curriculum does not preclude formal courses in religion as well. The courses in religion as such should serve to coordinate and give added meaning to the scattered references to religion in the other disciplines. Furthermore, the presence of a well-developed academic discipline of religion within the curriculum provides a standard of scholarly adequacy by which the incidental references to religion in other courses can be assessed. Such a discipline holds in check irresponsible allusions to religion by either its friends or its enemies. It helps to insure that the treatment of religion in the various academic fields will have regard both for relevance and for truth.

Religion as a dimension of other studies

Another way in which religion may belong to the curriculum is as an implicit dimension in the several areas of study. This differs from the previously discussed incidental treatment of religion in not being concerned primarily with the cultural facts of organized religion but with the religious meaning inherent in the specialized pursuits of learning. For example, in the study of English literature it may prove necessary to deal objectively with the religious ideas of Milton or with the place of the Bible in Shakespeare, as cultural facts. But these religious aspects are different from the quality of spiritual outlook implicit in literary study. Milton and Shakespeare—or for that matter writers who make no explicit reference to religion—can be read with an eye for the revelation of meaning and truth at the deepest levels. One can discern in the great works of literature symbolic portrayals of the human situation in all its glory and tragedy. The written word may also be recognized as a great liberator of creative imagination and hence as a means of realizing spirituality and self-transcendence.

Or consider the study of mathematics. There is little of an explicitly religious nature which is relevant to the purposes of this discipline. It may be of passing interest to mention the religious character of the ancient Pythagorean brotherhood and to refer to sacred numbers in the symbolism of religion, but no such incidental facts about religion are necessary to the understanding of mathematics itself or even to becoming a well-educated person. But the nature of one's personal concern in engaging in mathematical activity *is* of great importance both in understanding the true nature of this discipline and in general educational development. For example, it makes a profound difference whether one regards mathematics as merely a tool to be employed for personal pleasure and advantage, or as an opportunity to pursue truth, to catch glimpses of rational perfection, and to enter imaginatively into the citadel of order and possibility. The latter alternatives represent mathematics studied in the light of its inherent religious dimensions rather than as a technical pursuit.

Every subject in the curriculum has its religious dimensions, because by definition of ultimacy there is no human activity which in principle lies outside the domain of ultimate concern. Each department of academic study reflects in its own way the spiritual situation of those who pursue it. History, language, the arts, natural and social science—all of the disciplines—manifest fundamental beliefs and values in characteristic ways. It is the function of a deeply religious approach to these studies to point to the possibilities of realizing ultimate meanings in them rather than remaining satisfied with a limited and conventional perspective.

The meaning of religion as a dimension in other studies cannot be stated briefly and precisely. Nor is there any simple formula which describes how to "make the curriculum religious" in this fundamental sense. The religious dimensions implicit in the various studies can only be understood as the teacher gains skill in interpreting any and every human enterprise in the light of convictions about importance, value, meaning, beginnings, ends, totality, and relationships. The one requirement is a mature and fundamentally religious outlook, which can become effective in any segment of the educator's work.

Religion as a dimension of other studies is appropriate in the curriculum of all schools, public or private, at every level of instruction. The religious question in the fundamental sense is inescapable. All studies carry with them certain spiritual presuppositions. The educator's obligation is to examine and to improve the spiritual quality, and this constitutes an invitation to consider every subject in the curriculum from a religious perspective.

Finally, just as the study of religion as a separate organized discipline may make the incidental references to religion in other disciplines more relevant and authentic, so may it also contribute to a more adequate perception of the religious dimensions implicit in other studies. Hence the implicit concern for religion throughout the curriculum does not diminish but rather enhances the significance of the systematic study of religion as such. Each approach serves to enrich and confirm the other.

Explicit worship

Each of the foregoing ways of including religion in the curriculum has been concerned with the program of formal courses. Broadly conceived, the curriculum includes other kinds of learning experiences to which religion may be pertinent. One of these is corporate worship. While the study of religion in courses emphasizes the intellectual aspects of religion, the practice of worship is concerned also with emotional and volitional aspects. The importance of worship consists in the fact that religion can never be truly understood merely as idea. Devotion, dedication, decision, and concern are of its essence. Intellectual belief alone, no matter how sincerely held, is not sufficient to constitute a living faith. The formal act of worship symbolizes the personal involvement of the entire self in the life of faith.

Public worship further serves as a reminder and reinforcement of the social aspect of religion. The community is an important factor in creating and sustaining faith. Commitments not shared with others are not likely to prove as effectual in the conduct of life as those which have communal sanction. Also the meaning of symbolic acts is greatly enhanced when they are corporate rather than solitary.

In order that all students shall have the benefit of worship experience, some schools require participation in corporate services of worship. According to the view held in these schools, religion in the full and active sense cannot be understood merely by study and observation or even by private prayer; one must take part in the actual offering of corporate devotions.

There are three problems connected with such a system of compulsory participation in worship. By far the most crucial is the fact that compulsion in worship is a contradiction in terms. True worship is a free offering of the self in praise, contrition, and love. It cannot be demanded. A student can be required to attend services of worship and perhaps even to go through the motions of worshipping, but he cannot be required to worship. If he goes unwillingly and resentfully, he will learn not devotion but hypocrisy. He will become expert at giving the appearance of piety while his heart is far away. The experience of compulsion sometimes educates the student against religion, so that when he is once again at liberty he will dissociate himself from its organized expressions. Or, perhaps more unfortunately, he may come to accept the outward forms of devotion as the substance of religion itself, never realizing the deep concerns which are its true essence.

In justice to the practice of requiring worship it should be noted that in many cases even students who have participated against their will in time come to appreciate deeply and sincerely the practices of corporate devotion. Without the requirement to engage in worship it is possible that this highly prized habit of life would never have been acquired. Many of the most valuable lessons would not be learned without the insistence of the more mature, who know from experience how significant certain attainments may later become. Even the presently meaningless, mechanical performance of formal acts *may* provide the basis for subsequent experiences of profound personal import.

The second problem presented in requiring common worship is the diversity of liturgical traditions usually represented in the student body. Ways of worship are so specific and faithfulness to established formulae is so important that even minor departures from the customary may be a source of confusion and distraction. In dealing with this problem several approaches are open. The liturgy used may be that of one of the established religious denominations—in the case of a church-related school normally that of the sponsoring denomination—and students with other affiliations may be expected to adjust to this standard. Another approach is to construct a special non-denominational form of service either composed of elements from several major traditions or especially created for the school situation. These eclectic and artificial symbolic structures generally lack real integrity and vitality. A meaningful service cannot be pieced together with bits from other wholes. Furthermore, good liturgy grows out of the long experience of a worshipping community; it cannot be made to order. Another attempt at solution is to use several different forms of worship in succession, thus giving the students experience in a number of the traditions represented. When this is done, the values of regularity and continuity, so important for genuine, wholehearted devotion, are lost and the congregation tends to regard the services as performances to be observed rather than as occasions for personal participation.

The problem of diversity can, of course, be solved by providing separate services for each tradition represented. The feasibility of this approach depends on the size of the school, the personnel available for leadership, and the existence nearby of places of worship which students can attend. The objection usually offered to this solution is that worship becomes a means of continuing and accentuating ties beyond the school which separate one from another, rather than a corporate act unifying students in a common devotional life.

The third problem connected with compulsory worship is that of legality. This has already been discussed in Chapter

3 and need not be considered further here. It suffices merely to repeat that the question only pertains to public schools, not to private ones, and that though adherence to a principle of church–state separation would clearly prohibit any acts of explicit worship in public education, there are in practice either widespread breaches of that principle or interpretations of the law which lend official sanction to certain kinds of corporate religious devotions in public schools.

Instead of including worship in the curriculum as an experience required of all students it may be presented as a voluntary activity. The great gain in this approach is in fostering sincerity in worship. The spirit of a service is transformed when the participants come to it freely rather than to fulfill a requirement. But this spirit, precious though it is, is purchased at a price. Some students never come to know the meaning and satisfaction of worship simply because they have never become sufficiently accustomed to it, by involuntary exposure, to know what they are rejecting or neglecting. Often the student's prior experience of worship has been unrewarding, so that he shuns corporate devotions at school without even seeking to discover whether the new provisions might not be more congenial than the old. In some cases the student's reluctance to engage in worship is merely one aspect of becoming free from the authority of parents and reflects no real hostility to organized religion; but in absenting himself from public worship he breaks a habit of participation which may be difficult to re-establish. Often, too, the pressure of other activities causes the student who would normally engage in worship to neglect it; an attendance requirement would protect him against this betrayal of his own best judgment.

One possible effect of making public worship voluntary is loss of a sense of corporate unity in the school. When the entire academic community engages in devotional acts together, a bond of kinship may be established which has profound beneficial consequences for the morale and the spiritual health of the school. When some worship and the rest do not, whatever unity of spirit the school possesses must rest on other grounds and find other modes of expression. These other sources of unity may, of course, be more religious in the fundamental sense than participation in formal worship.

Finally, voluntary worship has the same effect as elective courses in religion, of encouraging an essentially superficial conception of religion as a specialized pursuit which is engaged in by those who have a taste for it, rather than as a matter of ultimate concern governing the outlook and disposition of the whole of life.

Implicit worship

In explicit worship, whether required or voluntary, the symbols of the organized religious traditions are employed, and the activity is recognized and designated as worship. There may be other occasions not ordinarily considered religious, where an implicit rather than an explicit kind of worship takes place. Such occasions constitute another way in which religion becomes a part of the school curriculum. Implicit worship occurs whenever a situation calls forth an active expression of ultimate concern, for example, in love, reverence, devotion, and the sense of mission. There are moments in the life of the school when the sacred appears within the ordinary, when the everyday activity becomes transfigured by a vision of extraordinary significance and high purpose.

Every school has its corporate celebrations, with appropriate symbols of the supreme goals to which the academic community is committed. Persons in solitude and in company often give praise, offer thanksgiving, confess, repent, implore, intercede, and resolve—all in the name and for the sake of truth and righteousness—without explicit use or acknowledgment of customary religious forms. Whenever the heart is lifted up, the affections purified, the will energized for good, the intellect illumined, whenever one is suffused with fresh life, in every moment of true inspiration, worship takes place. Such worship need not wait for special times and places, knows no difference of public or private school nor law of separation, requires no approved formulae, and respects no subject matter divisions.

Religion in the activity program

In addition to study and worship, religion may become a part of the course of study through the activity program. Even though such student activities do not usually take place in classroom or in chapel, they nevertheless do belong to the curriculum, broadly conceived as the whole complex of learning opportunities provided under school auspices. Some of the activity groups are explicitly and avowedly religious in the traditional sense, as, for example, the Student Christian Associations, Hillel Clubs, or Newman Clubs. Other groups, such as language clubs, Future Teachers clubs, and International clubs, are not religious in name but may provide opportunities for expressing ultimate concern even more effectively than the explicitly religious organizations. That is to say, the same duality of explicit and implicit religiousness that was discussed above in connection with courses and with worship applies also to the activity program.

The special value of the student clubs lies in their voluntary and informal character. They reflect real and spontaneous interests. They provide opportunities for the exercise of initiative and for free experimentation. Since the students usually take major responsibility for the conduct of these activities, they frequently learn much that they cannot acquire from the formal curriculum. Because religion in the inward sense involves freedom and responsibility of commitment, the activity program is peculiarly well suited to growth in the life of faith.

Frequently the voluntary student associations provide for study and for participation in worship. These experiences sometimes supplement corresponding opportunities or requirements in course work or in official services of worship. In other cases, where religious instruction and practice are neglected or forbidden in the school itself, the student clubs constitute the sole school-related channels for explicit religious participation. In these latter institutions a well-developed student organization program is, from the religious standpoint, especially imperative.

Student clubs have the further value of giving expression to legitimate and mutually enriching individual and group differences within the school community. Unity of objectives, program, and spirit is important for the school, but so are individual freedom and variety. It is the latter which are most admirably served by the activity program. It is often difficult or impossible to do full justice in courses and in school-sponsored services of worship to the varieties of faith represented by the students. Religious clubs are particularly well adapted to fill this need.

The religious activity program is important in two further respects. First, it helps to supply a matrix of personal warmth and social intimacy in which faith may grow. Student clubs thus emphasize the social and recreational avenues for religious development. Secondly, most student groups provide opportunities for putting faith to work in acts of service. Young people are likely to be dissatisfied with any religion which traffics only in concepts and rites. They want to put their concern to the proof of deeds. Many a student, immersed in the accumulation of knowledge through the formal curriculum, tends to lose the sense of practical relevance in his studies. The service projects of student organizations—such as clothing drives, work camp experiences, and political action programs—provide ample means for the concrete implementation of personal and social ideals and thus for the expression of religious faith in action.

Counseling and religious growth

Another phase of the curriculum to which religion is relevant is the program of guidance and counseling. Conventionally, religion is comprised of intellectual beliefs, ritual activity, and institutional affiliation, but in inner essence it is the core of personal being. Deeper than its rational and social aspects, the seed or center of religion is the orientation of the self to the fundamental questions of existence. In principle the function of the counselor is to give needed assistance to the student as he faces the deep personal issues of life. Academic courses, services of worship, and activity programs may all promote personal growth at profound levels, but none of these kinds of curricular provision is designed specifically for the individual student in formulating his own life-making decisions. Concern for the unique person in his search for responsible orientation is the special contribution of counseling. The guidance program is predicated on the principle that course work, attendance at public functions, and participation in group activities are not sufficient to fulfill some of the student's crucial needs, and that these should be supplemented by opportunities for individual, face-to-face consultation with a mature, sensitive, sympathetic, and trusted counselor.

Counseling is, of course, not necessarily done only by specially designated personnel or in special times set apart for this work. Every teacher and administrator is called upon to give personal guidance on occasion. Some do most of their teaching by the method of individual counseling. From the standpoint of curriculum what is important is simply that opportunity be given somewhere in the program for personal consultation by the student with competent advisers.

Much counseling is not religious either explicitly or implicitly. The matters discussed are not related to organized religion nor are they of ultimate concern. Counseling is religious when the student seeks help either on some problem of belief or conduct connected with his church or on an issue of ultimate concern—of life-and-death importance—whether or not expressed in traditional religious terms. Some counseling is religious in name and in auspices, but involves matters which do not go to the heart of personal orientation and thus are not religious in any fundamental sense. In other cases none of the usual religious language is used, but the matters dealt with are in the realm of comprehensive orientation and crucial decision, and hence are religious in fact though not in name.

The quality of religious counseling is a function of the counselor's personal adequacy. To deal effectively with the springs of another's selfhood the counselor must himself have pondered long and earnestly the deep issues of his own existence. He must also possess the wisdom to read the signs of personality with discernment; for example, he should not always identify verbal assertion with inner intention. He must also be aware of his own technical limitations as a counselor and be ready to refer the student to specialists when their assistance is needed.

Religion and the curriculum as a whole

In the foregoing paragraphs the principal ways in which religion may appear in the curriculum have been described. In this concluding section the relevance of religion as ultimate concern to the curriculum as a whole will be considered. Curricula may be prepared with a view to ultimate values or with only superficial concern; between the results of these two approaches there are profound differences. Some of the characteristics of a religiously-grounded total curriculum will be described in the following paragraphs.

Vitality. Since importance and value are aspects of ultimacy, religious concern should produce a curriculum that has vital significance for the students. It should not include studies which have no demonstrable relevance to their lives. "Inert ideas," perhaps once bright with meaning but now honored only in traditional usage, should not be forced into unwilling and uninterested pupils. Curriculum is for man and not man for the curriculum. Studies are instruments of the good life, and unless materials to be learned have a clear role in the enhancement of this life they do not belong in the curriculum. In theological terms, God is of the living, not of the dead. He is the source and ground of *being,* not of emptiness.

From the religious standpoint, therefore, the curriculum should be prepared with deliberate attention to its life-giving qualities. Whatever proves to be permanently without interest or importance to those who study it ought to be eliminated, and a persistent effort should be made to include materials which invite continuing and growing enthusiasm and devotion.

Centrality. Ultimate religion is also dedicated to depth as opposed to superficiality. Hence a religiously-based curriculum provides an education in fundamentals, or matters of *central* significance. Studies which go to the roots are preferred to those which merely gather the fruits of learning. The student must not merely have a show of knowledge; he should understand deeply and thoroughly. Learning should become *revelation.* The student then becomes not merely a knower but a "seer." Matters which are peripheral or trivial, which lead to no further insight, and which do not go to the heart of real human problems, are to be avoided in favor of key ideas which open wide vistas of new understanding.

In the light of this principle, it is better to teach a few basic disciplines well than to present a great variety of miscellaneous subjects of secondary significance. Of every subject it should be asked: Will the understanding of this provide the student with continuing resources of new insight, or will it merely add further items to the stockpile of occasionally useful information or skill?

Scope. Since comprehensiveness is another aspect of ultimacy, a curriculum constructed on religious principles should be inclusive in scope. While this requirement might seem to be in conflict with that of depth mentioned in the preceding paragraph, it actually is not. Inclusiveness of scope is not so much a quantitative ideal as a qualitative one. It means openness to any and every domain of human experience. Deeply significant ideas are central in that they lead outward to a wide range of other related concerns. Scope in the curriculum means that studies are not arbitrarily limited to a narrow specialized field, but that the learner is given a lively sense of the boundless network of truths within which all particular elements of knowledge find their place.

The religious outlook is critical of all closed, constricted schemes. It refuses to be satisfied with any system of knowledge as complete and final. It demands openness to new ideas, acknowledging the infinitude of reality and of possible knowledge. Hence the religiously based curriculum is *liberal,* not in the sense that it comprises only the traditional "liberal studies," as contrasted with practical and vocational preparation, but in that it sets no bounds to the search for understanding, freeing the learner to follow the path of truth wherever it leads.

Integrity. Finally, the curriculum constructed in a religious spirit has integrity or wholeness. This quality presupposes centrality and scope—depth of understanding and comprehensiveness of concern—but also something more, namely, awareness of interrelationships among the constituent parts of the course of study. From this viewpoint the curriculum is not a series of isolated and unrelated subjects. Academic departments are not regarded as completely autonomous disciplines, without connection with each other or with life beyond library, laboratory, or classroom. Education is regarded as the nurture of whole persons through participation in a *uni*verse of interconnected experiences.

The religious aim of integrity in the curriculum stands in opposition to the frequent conception of the program of study as the completion of certain specified separate course units, each representing a complete and self-contained learning capsule. While the value of distinctions and specialties is not denied, under the religious view, channels of communication and of cooperative endeavor are kept open, and the enterprise of teaching and learning is regarded as an adventure toward wholeness of personal and corporate life, in which all teachers, scholars, and pupils are united.

Curriculum content and the spirit of teaching. Ultimate concern becomes effective only in the spirit which animates the actual work of teaching and never merely in the determination of course content and sequence. There is no mechanical way of guaranteeing ultimacy, through a schedule of subjects to be covered. *Any* subject can be taught with vitality, depth, openness, and integrity. However, course content and sequence planned in the light of these principles are likely to provide more effective vehicles for the religious spirit than curricula based on purely traditional or finite practical considerations.

5 RELIGION AND THE ADMINISTRATIVE PROCESS

THE conduct of education within the school depends not only upon teaching and curriculum but also upon the administrative process. Like all organized social institutions, the school requires a variety of officers who are responsible for its effective functioning. The numerous activities of the students and teachers must be coordinated, continuity of function in the face of staff changes must be insured, and facilities adequate to the realization of teaching objectives must be provided. The necessary administrative functions may be, and to a limited extent usually are, performed by teachers, or even on occasion by students, but for the most part special administrative officers such as superintendents, principals, presidents, deans, supervisors, department heads, directors of admissions, and registrars are appointed to take care of these tasks.

Normally the administrative officers do not actually create basic school policy. They are charged with the execution of policy formulated by the responsible governing body such as the school board or the trustees. The executives also make all necessary administrative policy, that is, decisions necessary to the effective fulfillment of delegated responsibilities.

Thus they are of great importance in determining the nature of the learning experiences provided.

Our task now is to examine the religious foundations of the administrative process. In certain respects—especially in church-connected schools—the administrator is concerned with the relation of his school to organized religion. In addition to these obviously religious aspects of his work there are perspectives on administration which are religious in the inner and fundamental sense. We turn first to these basic religious perspectives, reserving the more traditional aspects for comment later in the chapter.

The spirit of the school

Administrators are to a large extent instrumental in creating the spirit of the school. They do much to set the dominant tone, the basic outlook and attitude, of the academic community. In some schools there is a pervasive undercurrent of fear and suspicion, in other schools a spirit of confidence and trust. Sometimes the mood is one of expectancy and excitement, sometimes it is one of discouragement and boredom.

Administrative officers have an effect on the spirit of an institution largely in proportion to the scope of their responsibilities. It follows that the superintendent, president, or principal—the chief executive officer of the school—usually has the most decisive influence. His standards and aspirations become effective throughout the school as they are translated day by day into the fabric of concrete decision. The spirit of the institution is largely a reflection of the system of values cherished by the persons in whom authority is vested. That which is supremely important to the administrator is made evident in the content and manner of executive action. Thus the administrator's actual religious faith—his ultimate concern—finds articulation in the quality of life within the school. His spiritual condition is not merely his own affair, nor of consequence only to a small circle. It is a powerful factor in establishing the spiritual situation of the whole institution.

The spiritual responsibility of the administrator may be summarized in the observation that *leadership is inspiration.* To lead is to breathe a spirit into an institution. An administrator is effective as a leader—whether for good or for evil—in proportion as he is able to actualize his fundamental convictions in the life of the school as a whole. It follows that the nature of the administrator's spiritual life—his basic ideals and commitments—is not a matter of indifference, and that the quality of the entire school's life may be at stake in the question of the leader's religious outlook.

The integrity of the educational program

The spirit of a school is its organizing principle—that which gives integrity to the whole. An educational program is integral when it is not merely a haphazard assortment of separate elements, but rather when each part has its appropriate function within a complex unity. Integrity implies a unifying idea, a hierarchy of values whereby every element is given its due emphasis.

Administrative officers are chiefly responsible for creating and maintaining the integrity of the institution. They are in the best position to see the work of the entire school in its true proportions and thus to contribute to the effective interrelating of components. This establishing of relationships is one aspect of religious concern. To help bring association out of isolation is part of the approach to ultimacy. The administrator has the spiritual task of linking students, teachers, service staff, and community, together with cultural and material resources, into a living social organism.

But integrity in its full meaning involves more than unity. An educational program can be well articulated, yet narrow in scope. There are mechanical and unimaginative ways of organizing a school which are the antithesis of ultimacy. Integrity, religiously conceived, presupposes wide perspective, breadth and inclusiveness of interest. It is not the unity of closedness, self-containment, and self-satisfaction, but a comprehensive unity in intention and concern. Thus from the religious standpoint the administrator views his school in relation to the entire human and cosmic drama and not merely as an independent enterprise. He seeks to understand the function of his institution within the larger society and as contributing to the development of the entire family of man.

In religious perspective school administration requires vision. The school is seen as more than this limited, inadequate human organization. By the power of imagination it is recognized as a link in the chain of creative process, an instrument for the progressive embodiment of ideals, and a matrix for soulmaking. Such vision is not, of course, the sole prerogative of administrators. They are, however, in a special way responsible for the wholeness of the educational enterprise and to an unusual extent obligated not only to establish harmonies within the institution but also to relate its activities to the most inclusive realities and ideals.

Power and authority

Administration may be defined as the exercise of social power. Every institution exists to fulfill certain specified social purposes, and these can be realized only as the organization operates in a determinate and harmonious fashion. Indecisiveness and internal conflict reduce institutional effectiveness. The function of administration is to maintain an organization in efficient operating condition. This is achieved through the exercise of social power, involving a principle of authority to which obedience is due. The administrator's responsibility is to see to it, within the limits set to his authority by higher powers, that the proper work of the institution is done.

The school administrator, in particular, has authority to secure the effective discharge of educational obligations. He occupies a specific and usually well-defined position within a power structure. His office is vested with definite powers which set the boundaries of his responsibility and influence.

The exercise of social power is a matter of religious significance. The administrator takes upon himself the authority in some degree to direct and control the lives of other people. In so doing he establishes his convictions as a source of meaning and of being for others. That is, his decisions affect not only himself but determine to some extent the quality of life for those over whom he has authority. The higher in the power structure the administrator rises, the wider becomes the scope of his authority and the more fateful his administrative decisions. In proportion to his power also is his temptation to play God, by considering his authority as absolute and infallible. Thus the administrator is in special need of the grace of humility, so that he may see himself in true proportion within the whole scheme of things rather than as himself the very wellspring of life for those above whom he stands in the power hierarchy.

There are, in fact, at least four sources in which the administrator's authority may be considered grounded. These four are associated with quite different approaches to the administrative task and reflect utterly different spiritual situations.

The autonomous executive. First, the administrator may regard himself as the source of his authority. He does not regard himself as genuinely responsible to any other authority nor as rightfully subject to any law beyond his own will and intention. To be sure, he recognizes the limitations which are thrust upon him by the social and physical situation in which he must live. These he accepts as factors which must be taken into account in distinguishing between what is and what is not possible or practical. Also he is generally conscious that he derives his power from those who have appointed him to office (e.g., to a board of trustees), and that to continue in office he must take account of their wishes and demands. But all of these factors of limitation and subordination are regarded by the autonomous executive as unavoidable circumstances which set the conditions for his exercise of personal initiative. The good, he thinks, is what he decides. The perfect world would be one which he would wholly create. Unfortunately, there are other people who also want to make the world in their own way, and so it is necessary to compromise, and to give other people their own kingdoms—some small, some large—in which they may rule. In this competitive scheme each person strives for the greatest possible authority, taking and holding whatever power he can secure.

From the standpoint of ultimacy this attitude is idolatrous, in that the autonomous power figure in principle affirms himself as rightful creator of the world, and thus as a god. He does not acknowledge any authority over himself, by right, but only by necessity in a world where others also contend for absolute power. By considering himself as the center and source of meaning he is prevented from freely establishing deeper and more sensitive relationships with other persons and things. Thus by absolutizing his own claims he becomes ever farther removed from true ultimacy.

The representative. A second type of administrator is at the opposite extreme from the autonomous executive. Instead of regarding himself as a primal source of authority, he considers his function as a purely representative one. He acknowledges the authority of those who have appointed him (e.g., the school board) and exercises the powers delegated to him in such a way as to fulfill their intentions. He does not act on his own initiative, nor does he assume any personal responsibility for the policy which he puts into operation. His sole responsibility is the derived one of carrying out faithfully the orders received from above.

Representative administration escapes the idolatry of the autonomous will. It also takes account of the larger context of human relationships within which the school must be conducted. The school executive should not attempt to fashion a self-contained educational microcosm, without genuine concern for the demands and aspirations of other persons. In this respect the dutiful representative of those who make school policy is closer to the religious ideal of relatedness than is the autonomous executive.

On the other hand, limitation of action to the faithful execution of orders from above is a means of escaping proper ultimate responsibility. If the policies which the administrator carries out are merely the expression of the self-will of the policy-makers, then by his executive action he merely confirms and entrenches their worship of self. By becoming an object within the circle of their egocentricity, he not only more tightly shuts the doors against wider and deeper insights but he also denies his own spiritual nature. Since his birthright is freedom, he cannot remain true to himself in acting wholly as the agent for another. He is called to the service of what is to him of supreme worth and not to the obedient implementing of the values of someone else. In this respect the autonomous executive, in affirming his freedom and personal responsibility, is more faithful to the religious ideal than the representative. Both miss ultimacy, though by different paths, the former by remaining within the circle of his own self-sufficient finitude, the latter by refusing the claims of a fully personal commitment.

The legalist. A third type of administrator, the legalist, finds the source of authority neither within himself nor in other persons above him in the power structure but in a set of rules or principles. Authority resides in the law, and the executive's task is to insure the effective implementation of the relevant rules. The legalist administrator does not create the laws, as does the autonomous executive, nor does he regard them simply as expressions of the will of the policy-makers, as does the representative. The law has its own justification, in reason and experience, and hence commands universal assent and obedience. With respect to the law the administrator and those who are subordinate to him in the power structure are on a par; all are subject to the same law. The administrator is simply charged with the special duty of securing compliance with the regulations. He is an officer of the law.

The exercise of power by reference to law provides protection against the arbitrary imposition of personal will. General principles are beyond the caprice and partiality of the individual ego. They provide a foundation for universality in the conduct of human affairs, free from the accidents of time and circumstance. For this reason the legalistic administrator, as a "man of principle," has been commonly associated with religious faith. The religious traditions contain moral and ritual regulations obedience to which is considered evidence of personal piety. These attitudes have often been carried over, either in substance or by analogy, to the administrative sphere, providing religious justification for the legalistic approach.

Still, legalistic administration easily falls under judgment at the bar of ultimacy. For a rule or principle strictly and literally applied may become an occasion for idolatry just as surely as the self-will of the autonomous administrator. In fact, the temptation is even greater for the man of principle because he may deceive himself and others by professing high-mindedness which is actually a cloak for his own power impulses. Despite his insistence on dedication to objective principles of right and justice, the fact remains that the rules which he affirms and defends have been chosen by him and hence may be as fully an expression of his personal will to power as the naked command of autonomous man.

Furthermore, administration by principle tends to become

impersonal. Human beings, in their uniqueness and freedom, become submerged in a sea of regulations. Abstractions of law become more important than persons. Traditional rules or rational generalizations may be applied in such a way as to do no justice to the irreducible singularity of particular individuals and occasions. Subservience to the letter of the law brings stagnation and death rather than creativity and vitality.

Thus the legalist in school administration may by the earnestness and efficiency of his endeavor reveal his concern for that which is not truly ultimate. He may choose as his authority for the exercise of power rules, principles, or laws which are only worthy of provisional and limited allegiance, and which themselves stand under the judgment of a higher power from whom such dignity as they possess is derived.

The servant of the most high. Consideration of the religious limitations of the three preceding conceptions of the administrator's source of authority leads to a final view of the administrator as a "servant of the most high." This expression is a symbol for administration guided by the canons of ultimacy, the general phrase "most high" allowing for a variety of alternative designations such as "God," "Truth," "the Good," or "the really Real," yet always with emphasis on that which is worthy of truly personal dedication or commitment rather than on abstract qualities.

In contrast with the autonomous executive, the servant of the most high aims not to fulfill his own will but that of another to whom he has pledged himself. But unlike the representative, he is not merely the servant of other persons who make policy, for the most high, who is the ground from which all authority springs, transcends all human authorities. Nor does the servant of the most high merely follow the letter of the law, since he knows that no rule fully expresses what is right for all persons and in every circumstance. He acknowledges that laws, like the men who formulate and use them, are fallible and at best a general guide to just behavior.

How, then, does the administrator as servant of the most high regulate his conduct? He exercises his power with full freedom and responsibility, not as furthering his own ambitions but as responding to the claims of right made upon him. He does not enclose this right within rules or precepts, because he understands the uniqueness of each new situation and the necessity for making every decision a fresh creative act in the light of the manifold circumstances. He acknowledges that the ultimate authority lies beyond him and that his role is to serve as far as possible as an agency through whom some truth may shine and some justice be done.

The spiritual quality of educational administration thus depends upon the source of authority acknowledged in the exercise of power within the social institution. The administrator himself, other persons, and legal principles all fall short of being ultimately trustworthy authorities. A mature religious faith is manifest in the administrator whose acts are performed in glad devotion to the most high, yet with humble acknowledgment that they are at best fragmentary fulfillments of the ultimate good, and with aspiration toward ever more perfect embodiments of the ideal.

Academic freedom

The problems of power and authority are nowhere more evident than in the matter of academic freedom. The freedom to teach and to learn are fundamental ideals of the academic community. They have their justification in part in the fact that knowledge can grow only when there is inquiry, and that *a priori* restrictions in the field of inquiry may hinder discovery. The morale of the school is also a factor. Teachers and students prize an atmosphere of respect for them as persons and of trust in the responsible execution of their academic tasks.

Beyond these practical logical and psychological justifications of academic freedom there is a basic religious principle, about the source of ultimate authority. In the final analysis the ideal of academic freedom is founded on the recognition that no person or organization can lay claim to final truth, but that all men and institutions stand under judgment of a Truth and a Right which are relevant to all finite formulations but forever beyond complete embodiment. Freedom is the social condition for acknowledging the infinitude of ultimate truth.

Academic freedom is an administrative problem because the organization, for whose efficient operation the administrator is responsible, must be conducted in accordance with certain definite rules which place limits upon teachers and students. Teaching and learning must occur within specified boundaries. Thus freedom is not absolute. The problem is how to draw the lines of necessary administrative limitation in such a way that the pursuit of the good and the true is aided rather than hindered.

The autonomous executive, the representative, and the legalist are all likely to infringe academic freedom, because they determine institutional procedures essentially on the basis of arbitrary authority. They deny the basic spirituality of the human being, in managing teachers and students as objects to be manipulated rather than as free self-determining subjects. The administrator who performs his functions with ultimate concern, on the other hand, recognizes his responsibility to a reality beyond himself, his policy-making superiors, and all principles of law. He is therefore in a better position to understand the importance of that openness to new truth which is the essence of academic freedom.

Sometimes academic freedom is abused by a teacher or student. It may become the occasion for personal license, in which sheer independence is sought rather than obedience to truth. The offender cries out in the holy name of academic freedom against any and all limitations and regulations. In effect he advocates a state of anarchy—usually, however, only as regards his own conduct—and hence seeks to nullify all administrative effectivness. The abuse of freedom may take the form of aggression, whereby the teacher uses his position as a vantage point for destructively attacking other persons, under the cloak of zeal for truth. Or the disease may appear as subversion, where the scholar with academic immunity works like a noxious parasite to undermine the social order which harbors and sustains him. In all of these misuses of academic freedom spirituality has become demonic in character. Powers of self-determination have been directed toward finite goods which exclude and negate other goods.

The predicament of the administrator is that there is no sure and simple way to distinguish the use from the abuse of academic freedom. How can he be certain that the anarchist or the subversive is not a true prophet proclaiming in the wilderness a just judgment on the existing order and the promise of a new day dawning? Can the administrator inerrantly distinguish a person who is simply anti-social from one who has a legitimate ground for protest and criticism? To make such judgments infallibly he would have to be a super-Prophet, if not the Almighty Himself. Since the administrator is neither of these, but is human, finite, and fallible, he must regulate the institution with due regard for practical and social necessities, but placing minimum restrictions on the manner of exercising well-defined teaching and learning functions. Whenever freedom is granted, it may be abused. To remove all possibility of misusing freedom, freedom itself would have to be destroyed, for freedom to err is inseparable from freedom to realize truth. The essential point is that though the academic community must live under some kind of social regulation, of which the administrator is custodian, this order should be framed with due provision for creative variation, experimentation and invention, wider scope, and new purposes, all of which belong to ultimate concern.

The selection of personnel

One of the most crucial of administrative responsibilities is the selection of personnel. The character of the school is not primarily defined by its institutional structure but by the quality of the persons who constitute its staff. Though the administrator may do much in the day-by-day performance of executive functions to create a dominant atmosphere or spiritual climate, by far the most decisive contribution he makes in this respect is in the making of faculty appointments. It is especially in these decisions that the actual nature of the administrator's basic faith is made evident. He may profess his devotion to certain values and pledge himself and his school to their realization, and yet by the nature of his faculty appointments he may betray a quite different pattern of real commitment. Another administrator may make no explicit faith-claims at all, but in the nature of his faculty selections clearly reveal his governing convictions.

In the selection of personnel there are, of course, several factors to be considered. There is the obvious practical consideration of matching institutional need with availability of suitable candidates. Most administrators are forced to settle for something less than their ideal in appointments simply because the field of available people is limited. Assuming a choice among candidates, what factors must the administrator weigh in making his selection? Three broad and interrelated considerations may be suggested.

First, there are factors of academic and professional competence. How well does the candidate know his subject? How good is his aptitude for work in his field? How adequate is his preparation in it? What skill has he acquired or does he give promise of acquiring in the work of teaching? These questions are not without relation to the administrator's religious faith, which, if it is really ultimate, must include respect for intellectual and professional excellence. The administrator who does not care deeply about the academic achievements of his faculty thereby denies that spirit of devotion to truth which is fundamental to the fulfillment of ultimate educational objectives. Still, concern for academic competence does not constitute the whole of the administrator's responsibility in selecting his faculty. These factors are necessary but not sufficient for ultimacy in choice of teaching staff; administrators who are interested only in scholarship and skill, though devoted to a kind of truth, are too narrow in their evaluations and hence are likely to fall short of the whole truth.

Hence a second set of factors, comprised under the general heading of "personal character," must be considered. Included in this category are such qualities as emotional maturity, poise, skill in establishing harmonious relationships with other people, modesty, patience, and courage. Personal characteristics have great significance for success in teaching and for the general morale and efficiency of the school. A teacher may be intellectually gifted and highly trained professionally and yet fail miserably as a teacher because of personality defects. The religiously oriented administrator is aware of these factors of personal character because he views the educational enterprise comprehensively and from the standpoint of personal commitment. He understands teaching not only as the communication of knowledge and skill but as the influence of life upon life, and he knows that the quality of personal existence imparted by the school is a function of the total orientation of those who teach, including emotional and moral characteristics as well as intellectual accomplishments.

In the third place, the administrator may also select his faculty with regard to their spirituality. He may believe that there are important factors which transcend academic ability and good personality. The problem is how to define and assess spirituality. One method is to use formal religious affiliation and profession of faith as criteria. This approach is simple and direct. It may be appropriate in church-related schools where the teacher's success and satisfaction may be affected by the nature of his connection with organized religion. It may be less appropriate in cases where the school is non-sectarian or secular. In fact, there are laws in some states which forbid the use of any religious test (in the conventional sense) as a qualification for teaching in a public institution. Such regulations presuppose that religious belief and affiliation are a private concern and that they have no bearing on the teacher's ability to perform. This assumption is justified only when religion is conceived as a special and separable pursuit rather than as ultimate concern.

Unfortunately, since religious affiliation often does have little relation to the major values of the teacher's life, it is a poor criterion of spirituality. The prospective faculty member may be a faithful church member and a firm believer and yet have so compartmentalized his piety that it has scant effect on his life-governing convictions. His "spirituality" in that case is conventional and unspiritual. Genuine spirituality cannot be ascertained from church membership or declaration of belief. Its assessment requires religious awareness by the administrator himself, if he is to recognize it in another. Typical signs of ultimate concern are deep interest in teaching as a vocation, joy in creating, a profound yearning for excellence, contagious enthusiasm, eagerness to learn and to share the fruits of discovery with others, and basic satisfaction with life united with a vivid expectancy of still greater goods to come. The true spirituality of the teacher is measured by the ultimacy of his concern. Thus, any characteristics, such as those just cited, that yield evidence of a life committed to the highest values, deepest insights, and most comprehensive relationships are criteria of spirituality. These qualities are actually not separable from those of academic competence and excellence of personal character, but are their wellsprings and the promise of their consummation.

Counseling and guidance

In addition to the general administrative functions which govern the school as a whole, there are specialized offices in which administration is made personally and individually relevant. Deans, officers for admissions and placement, and various types of counselors—psychological, vocational, and religious—offer services which though usually classified as administrative are in many respects closer to teaching. Counseling and guidance may, in fact, provide a more adequate opportunity for teaching and learning than most classroom situations.

From the religious standpoint several approaches to guidance may be distinguished, following in some respects the analysis of general administrative authority made above. First, guidance may be considered as authoritative direction. The counselor ascertains the student's problem and then prescribes for him the right course of conduct, just as a physician prescribes the suitable treatment for a bodily ailment. While this method has the merits of definiteness and apparent effectiveness, it submerges the uniqueness and freedom of the student, who becomes dependent upon the will of the counselor. The adviser is tempted to treat the student as an object, and by exercising authority over him to bring him into the orbit of the counselor's ego rather than helping the student to establish a way and an identity of his own.

A second approach to counseling is to consult regulations. This belongs within the category of legalistic administration discussed above. Each case is decided in the light of rulings and precedents. Difficulties arise when (as frequently happens) the rules do not cover the case. Since each situation and every person are different, the literal application of regulations is likely to prove either unsatisfactory or impossible. It is a mechanical, impersonal approach, which does scant justice to the essentially personal and intrinsically religious nature of most situations calling for guidance.

Psychological tests provide a powerful diagnostic instrument for the counselor. Their use constitutes in effect a third guidance method. The counselor using this approach would rely primarily neither upon his own wisdom and experience nor upon rules and regulations, but would use the scientific tests as a major basis of diagnosis and prescription. Because the adviser's private prejudices are thus minimized, the student is less likely to fall prey to the demands of the counselor's autonomous ego. However, there is no guarantee of objectivity, since the choice of the tests administered and their interpretation and individual application reflect the adviser's predispositions. While guidance by the use of tests does permit greater accuracy of individual judgment based on large experimental populations, it is in the last analysis an impersonal approach, founded upon statistical averages and upon the probable repetition in the future of past patterns of behavior. Though they may be valuable as an accessory instrument, psychological tests alone cannot do justice to the spiritual demands of the moment of personal decision.

Some counseling is explicitly religious in approach. The student's problem is assessed in the light of the religious beliefs of the student, of the adviser, or of both. Standard religious practices, such as prayer, Bible reading, attendance at church, and performance of works of charity may be prescribed. Some times these methods are of great value. Under the conditions of modern secular society, however, they often degenerate into stereotyped forms of behavior having little relation to the student's actual needs. Like the approaches which are not explicitly religious, religious counseling may also become legalistic or a device of the authoritarian personality.

In counseling and guidance with deep religious foundations use is made of the valuable features in all of the foregoing approaches. There are occasions when direct advice is appropriate. All counseling must also have regard for the rules by which the life of the academic community is governed. Psychological tests may provide helpful information, and traditional religious ideas and activities sometimes afford the best access to the student's innermost springs of life. But from a fundamental religious standpoint none of these approaches alone, nor any combination of them, suffices. For counseling is seen as an *occasion for creative decision in a unique interpersonal encounter.* Adviser and student are linked in mutual trust and responsibility in a common search for what is truly good. The counselor from his vantage point of greater maturity and deeper knowledge offers to the student access to a wider world of possibilities. The student in turn provides the adviser with the incomparable privilege of sharing in the progressive actualizing of ideals and with the enlargement and testing of his own experience through intimate association with the unique other person. Moreover, the outcome of the guidance occasion is never assured or predictable. Each situation is open to surprises. Every decision is a moment of creation, for which no principle or code can supply any sure pattern. In working out the student's problems, light on the path is gratefully received, but always with the recognition that every solution is but partial, and that each step leads on both to new opportunities and to new perplexities. Thus guidance in the religious spirit does not presume to supply final and correct answers, but to give assistance, through personal association in the counseling situation, in the never-finished task of manifesting goodness in the finite, concrete realities of human life. This is worship.

Ceremonial acts

In Chapters 3 and 4 some reference was made to religion in the school in the form of acts of worship. It was pointed out that leadership in ritual acts is one of the ways in which religion may be ingredient in the teacher's work, and that experiences of worship may be planned as part of the curriculum. A word is now in order concerning the relation of the administrator to ceremonial acts.

The chief administrative officer of the school is not only at the head of a power structure; he is also at the summit of a *symbolic* structure. In a sense he stands for the school as a whole. Ideally he is the visible embodiment of the spirit of the institution. This spirit is expressed in a variety of communal acts, and it is one of the major functions of the administrator to lead in the celebration of these corporate rites. In ecclesiastical language, the president or principal of a school is the bishop or chief priest of the community of scholars. He is the shepherd of the flock, the guardian of the sacred mysteries of academe. Every institution needs some outward evidence of its animating spirit, through explicit symbolic expressions. Its highest ideals are less secure if they reside merely in the silent aspirations of teachers and students and in the fragmentary realizations of accomplished deeds. They need also that intermediate mode of being, the *symbolic,* which is at once concrete and ideal, thus serving to bring the actual continually under the judgment and inspiration of the ideal and to keep the ideal always relevant to and available for the actual.

The ceremonial acts in some cases are traditionally religious in character, especially when the school has an official relationship to organized religion. Some institutions employ a special officer—the chaplain—to serve as leader in the religious services. As a professionally trained person he is supposed to have the particular skills necessary to perform these duties more effectively than could the ordinary layman. However, the use of professional religious leaders invites a compartmental view of religion rather than one in which the animating ideal of the entire institution is expressed. One of the best ways of fostering the latter outlook is for the general administrative officers—especially the head of the school—to conduct at least some of the religious services. In this way evidence is given, by symbolic act, of the official dedication of the school to the concerns of the religious tradition.

Many ceremonial acts are not religious in the traditional sense, yet because they do celebrate events of special significance for the academic community, they may have implicit religious significance. There are initiation ceremonies, at which new students and faculty members are inducted into the fellowship of the school. At the conclusion of the course of study comes the Commencement—the end which is also a beginning. Solemnity and joy mark occasions of remembrance for founders, benefactors, and academic saints and martyrs. Devotion and high resolve belong to services of dedication for new buildings or inauguration of new faculty and administrative officers. Honors awarded in recognition of scholarly achievement symbolize the values for which the institution stands. All such activities, involving as they do convictions about values, meanings, origins, and destinies, are opportunities for expressing ultimate concern. They mark occasions for symbolic representation of the governing commitments of the institution.

No small part of the administrator's responsibility is to plan and conduct such ceremonies. The quality of spiritual life in the school is to a degree dependent on the imagination and sincerity with which this task is fulfilled. Unhappy is the school where the administrator takes his ceremonial duties as routine obligations to be mechanically discharged. Blessed is the institution whose leaders regard the corporate symbolic acts as a high and sacred privilege.

Community relations

Finally, religious considerations enter into the question of the administrator's relationships with the community to which the school belongs. With respect to these community relations there are three main administrative responsibilities which should be noted.

First, there is the task of guarding the school against hostile and degrading influences by the larger community. An example is the demand for immediate results from education rather than for secure, long-term growth. The administrator must stand against the insistence on gross practicality when it is gained at the expense of depth and breadth of outlook. Again, in the name of truth anti-intellectual tendencies and threats to freedom of teaching and learning must be opposed. The administrator must champion the right and duty of the school to be true to its own high mission without subservience to external powers unacquainted or unsympathetic with the appropriate objectives of the academic enterprise. Apparently but not actually of a different character are many community pressures for the teaching of religion in the allegedly "godless" public schools. School officials should not only seek to correct false or misleading statements, if such there are, about the religious quality of the school program; they should also be zealous in preserving the freedom of the schools from sectarian bias and entanglement.

A second major responsibility of the administrator is to mediate to the school the sustaining, uplifting, life-giving influences from the larger community. Generous and faithful financial support may serve as tangible evidence of citizens' and benefactors' sense of responsibility for education and of their dedication to its purposes. The administrator, in carrying out his task of securing money grants, may also help those who give to see themselves as stewards of resources intended for wise, constructive uses—of which the support of education is an outstanding example. In addition to financial aid, the administrator should enlist the interest and cooperation of parents, alumni, and citizens in the program of the school. The resources of wisdom and inspiration within the environing community, available to the school if the right channels are established, are oftentimes exceedingly rich. Of special value to the school can be the active educational concern of the churches and synagogues in the community. The wise school administrator will be able to draw upon the spiritual energies of these sister institutions as he takes thought for the religious foundations of his own program. He will recognize and welcome the deep searching, the fervent expectation, and the serene trust which flow from a vital religious community and he will in appropriate ways encourage corresponding expressions of ultimate concern within the educational context.

In the third place, the school administrator has the prophetic obligation of interpreting the mission of the school to the larger community. He has a gospel to proclaim—the good news of release from ignorance, of passage from the darkness of prejudice to the light of understanding and acceptance, of freedom through knowledge and skill. His is a noble tradition to announce—a heritage of dedicated scholars, of devoted researchers, the abundant fruits of whose labors and the inspiration of whose high example have become our sacred trust. It is his privilege to demonstrate the role of the school in spiritual leadership through its free and unremitting exploration of all the heights and depths of human experience. For there is nothing in all the universe which properly lies beyond the concern of the school conscious of its religious task.